W9-BAM-819

8⁰⁰

ON BEING REFORMED

On Being Reformed

*Distinctive Characteristics
and Common Misunderstandings*

I. John Hesselink

SERVANT BOOKS
Ann Arbor, Michigan

Copyright © 1983 by I. John Hesselink

Cover photo by Historical Pictures Service, Chicago
Cover and Book Design by John B. Leidy

Available from Servant Publications, Box 8617, Ann Arbor,
    Michigan 48107

Printed in the United States of America
ISBN 0-89283-162-6

1 2 3 4 5 6 7 8 9 10   87 86 85 84 83

Library of Congress Cataloging in Publication Data

Hesselink, I. John, 1928-
    On being reformed.

    Bibliography: p.
    Includes index.
    1. Reformed Church. 2. Theology, Reformed Church.
3. Reformed (Reformed Church) I. Title.
BX9422.2.H47 1983   285   83-14441
ISBN 0-89283-162-6 (pbk.)

CONTENTS

Preface / vii
Introduction / 1

Misunderstanding One / 5
*That the word "Reformed" refers primarily
to denominations which bear that name, especially
those of Dutch origin.*

Misunderstanding Two / 9
*Since Reformed/Presbyterian Churches adhere to
creeds and confessions they are not biblical.*

Misunderstanding Three / 17
*That Reformed Churches are only those with a
Presbyterian church order.*

Misunderstanding Four / 21
*That Reformed/Presbyterian Churches are "low"
church and hence nonliturgical.*

Misunderstanding Five / 31
*That Reformed theology is rationalistic and
scholastic in its approach.*

Misunderstanding Six / 39
*That the doctrine of predestination is a creation
of and unique to the Reformed tradition.*

Misunderstanding Seven / 45
*That the doctrine of total depravity means that man
is worthless and capable of no good.*

Misunderstanding Eight / 51
*That the Reformed faith fosters a negative, legalistic
approach to the Christian life.*

Misunderstanding Nine / 57
*That the covenant concept produces a sense
of pride and exclusiveness.*

Misunderstanding Ten / 63
*That to be Reformed means to be indifferent or opposed
to the so-called "worldly" realm of culture,
economics, and politics and be concerned only
about the salvation of souls.*

Misunderstanding Eleven / 73
*That in the Reformed tradition the work and reality
of the Holy Spirit is ignored.*

Misunderstanding Twelve / 85
*That to be Reformed is to be anti-ecumenical
and frequently schismatic.*

On Being Reformed / 93
Some characteristic and distinctive emphases.

Bibliography / 113
Notes / 121
Index / 153

Preface

I AM BULLISH ON BEING REFORMED. It was not always so. If I had remained in the areas where my roots are—Grand Rapids, Michigan, and Pella, Iowa—I would not sing quite the same song, or at least not in the same way! When you are too close to something or someone, you tend to see only the warts. Distance and time give a more balanced perspective.

As a small boy, I knew of no other churches than Reformed and Christian Reformed. This was true both in Grand Rapids, where I was born, and in Leighton, Iowa (ten miles from Pella), where we moved when I was eight years old. Pella is a small town—now over 7,000 people—located forty miles southeast of Des Moines. Settled in 1847 by a group of Dutch immigrants led by the Reverend Hendrik Scholte, the town still reflects its Dutch Reformed heritage in distinctive religious and cultural ways. Since my father is a minister, I heard occasionally about other churches but I had no experience of them. I still have vivid recollections of the cultural-ecclesiastical shock of attending a Disciples of Christ church in Memphis, Tennessee, when I was twelve, an evening service in a Nazarene church in Illinois when I was fourteen, and very sophisticated services in Methodist, Congregational, and Episcopal churches in Evanston, Illinois, when, at sixteen, I spent a summer at Northwestern University. These other ecclesiastical worlds seemed extremely strange and alien.

Much more familiar and real were the little skirmishes between the two churches in Leighton (a town of about 125 people)—one Reformed, the other Christian Reformed. We argued about Christian schools, doctrinal purity, and use of the Dutch language. Above all, we argued about what one could properly do on Sundays besides go to church and read religious literature. Petty legalisms, a peculiar Dutch-American piety and church loyalty, and a strait-laced, very orthodox father (who has become more open and genial as he has aged) were the leading influences in my boyhood development as a Christian.

As I look back on those days, I am surprised that I never rebelled against this rather narrow version of the Christian faith—and the whole Reformed tradition! There were, fortunately, family friends and relatives—particularly a very literate, liberal uncle—who broadened my horizons and helped me see life whole. In any case, despite occasional questions and misgivings, I grew up as a loyal and generally appreciative son of the church. But I really did not have a very clear idea as to what was distinctive about the larger Reformed tradition as such. To be Reformed, at that point, meant basically: 1) to be orthodox; 2) to go to catechism; and 3) to go to church faithfully Sunday morning *and evening* and to honor the rest of the Sabbath Day in an appropriately sedate manner. That, needless to say, does not well represent the genius of the Reformed tradition! Even so, I shall always be grateful for this godly heritage and for the Reformed Church in America which brought it to me.

While in college and seminary,* I gradually was exposed to what made "us" different from "them" (i.e., all those other Christians of non-Reformed background). I was introduced to our Reformed "father," John Calvin. In my senior year at seminary, we made a cursory review of our standards of unity, but I was not especially impressed even by the Heidelberg Catechism. I had also married a Reformed minister's daughter who had also grown up in the Midwest, in a greater variety of places, but all traditional Reformed centers.

When we sailed to Japan as missionaries in 1953, we were

---

*All of my college training was spent at Central College in Pella, Iowa, a Reformed Church institution. My first year of theological training was spent at New Brunswick Seminary in New Jersey, the older of the two Reformed Church seminaries. My roommate was a liberal Methodist, and the environment was radically different from the conservative Calvinist milieu of the Pella area. I transferred to Western Seminary in Holland, Michigan, from which I graduated in 1953.

well-grounded theologically but had not had our inherited Reformed convictions tested and tried. Moreover, I had a bit of a minority complex, coming, as I did, from a very small town, a small college, a small seminary, and a small denomination, none of which were known in most parts of the United States.

Our missionary experience in Japan changed all that. We suddenly were exposed to missionaries of all stripes. There were liberals, who believed very little but had great compassion for the Japanese. There were fundamentalists, who seemingly had all the answers but cared little for the Japanese (except to add converts' scalps to their belts), or anyone else for that matter. Between these extremes was a growing circle of friends who both challenged and chastened us. They ranged from Southern Baptist and Pentecostal to Lutheran and Roman Catholic. This was enriched by deepening relationships with Japanese Christians, and non-Christians, and a host of international contacts during my three years of doctoral work in Basel, Switzerland. From the time I left Western Seminary as a young graduate in 1953 until the time I returned to become president of the seminary in 1973, I was in the United States only a little more than two years. During that time, and for extended periods, we worshiped with Southern Baptists, English Anglicans, American Lutherans, and Christian Reformed, along with local Japanese and Swiss churches.

This cultural and ecclesiastical diversity led into a period of intensive theological reflection and soul-searching. We were constantly being asked about our denomination and what we believed. There were occasions when I was charged with being liberal by fundamentalists (who regarded anyone with my kind of background and associations as suspect) and other occasions when I was called a fundamentalist by my liberal acquaintances. Thus, I was forced to reexamine everything that I had once assumed and taken for granted.

This process was aided and abetted by my more formal theological studies and professional associations. During my first year in Japan, I had the opportunity of studying with Emil Brunner, one of the most famous theologians of the time. He was a man whom I had read, admired, and attacked as a student. In the mysterious providence of God I soon found myself doing doctoral work in Basel with *the* theologian of our time, Karl Barth, regarded as liberal by some conservatives and as too orthodox by many liberals. I was also exposed to radical theologians such as Rudolph Bultmann and Fritz Buri, as well as more traditional scholars like Oscar Cullmann. More important I had come to a fresh appreciation of Calvin while teaching an English Bible class in a Tokyo high school. To my surprise, I found Calvin's commentaries more helpful—and more inspiring—than most of my contemporary commentaries. The result was that I ended up writing my doctoral dissertation on Calvin's concept of the law. It was something I would not have dreamed of while in seminary.

All of these experiences—academic, spiritual, ecumenical, and international—over a twenty-year span meant an increasing understanding and appreciation of what was distinctive and beautiful about the Reformed tradition. Much of what I learned and experienced is spelled out in the chapters of this book. In general, I discovered that we represent a middle way. We are neither liberal nor fundamentalist. At our best we share many liberal concerns (scholarly openness, social justice, etc.) as well as fundamentalist doctrines (a high view of the inspiration of scripture, the virgin birth, the second coming of Christ, etc.). We are neither high church nor low church, dispensationalists nor latitudinarians. Above all, we take scripture seriously—all of it, not simply those parts which appeal to evangelistic types, on the one hand, and social activists, on the other.

At the same time I was coming to appreciate our tradition more and more, I also came to see more clearly where we had failed to measure up to that tradition at its best. I learned a lot from my Southern Baptist, Lutheran, Anglican, Catholic, liberal, charismatic, and evangelical friends. I found that each of these traditions had something to offer, often something we were lacking. Every "misunderstanding" of the Reformed tradition is based on a degree of truth: where there is smoke, there is usually fire.

It may seem paradoxical that as I grew more appreciative (and less judgmental) of other traditions I became more enthused about my own. I recognize far better now than twenty years ago the foibles and failures of our particular expression of that tradition in the Reformed Church in America, but I also love and appreciate it now as never before.

Hence with a chastened realism and unashamed pride I gladly and gratefully acknowledge my Reformed heritage and tradition. The purpose of this book is to encourage and elicit a similar appreciation in those for whom being "Reformed" is new as well as others who have grown up in my tradition or in other branches of the broader Reformed tradition.

The Origin and Evolution of This Book

In September 1974, I was asked to give the convocation lecture at Western Seminary. A year earlier, I had given my inaugural lecture on the subject, "Toward a Seminary that Is Catholic, Evangelical, and Reformed."[1] The last point was the one dearest to me, but it had to be treated with such brevity that I hoped for an opportunity to expand on the theme. To treat the topic in a fresh way, I decided to deal with some of the misunderstandings I had encountered with wearying frequency. In that lecture, I touched on five and mentioned, in passing, that while preparing the lecture I had thought of another half dozen. About a month later, a representative of the seminary wives' organization asked me to cover the "misunderstandings" I had alluded to in my convocation address.

In this way a forty-minute lecture evolved into an eight-week course over the span of a year. In the process, I had shared it with seniors in a course on "Our Reformed Heritage" and was asked to teach in a nearby church. Since that time, I have taught the course in a host of Reformed churches in Western Michigan in as few as three and as many as ten weeks. I have also introduced all twelve "misunderstandings" in less than an hour to various adult Sunday School classes. It is a flexible format.

In 1980, a major revision was completed. I have further

revised the work in order to make it of wider interest and relevance, at the suggestion of Donald Bloesch of Dubuque Seminary and Philip Tiews of Ann Arbor. I am grateful to them for their helpful input. Though this book is intended for a much wider and more diverse audience, it is still a rather personal statement which arises out of and reflects my own experience and denominational background. I have discovered, however, that sabbatarianism and a narrow denominational outlook, for example, are not limited to Midwesterners and members of my denomination!

In the summer of 1980, I was invited to give these lectures to the Reformed/Presbyterian fellowship within The Word of God community in Ann Arbor, Michigan. Some who attended those lectures were not from the Reformed tradition. The staff of Servant Books expressed an interest in the material. I am particularly indebted to Jim Manney, the managing editor, without whose persistence, patience, and encouragement this project might never have come to fruition.

Finally, I want to express appreciation to several of my colleagues at Western Seminary who have read one or more chapters at various stages of development and have contributed constructive criticisms: Donald Bruggink, Eugene Heideman (now Secretary for World Missions, RCA), Christopher Kaiser, and Eugene Osterhaven. I am also indebted to two members of our staff, Dorothy Steketee and Harriet Bobeldyk, who typed the first drafts, and to Eleanor Hoffman, who typed all of the successive editions.

I. John Hesselink
Western Theological Seminary
Holland, Michigan

Lent, 1983

Introduction

APPROXIMATELY FIFTY YEARS AGO, a little book was published in Germany with the title *Was heisst reformiert?* (What Is the Meaning of Reformed?).[1] The author, Wilhelm Niesel, was to become the foremost Calvin scholar in Germany and eventually the president of the World Alliance of Presbyterian and Reformed Churches. He indicates that he wrote the book because the word *Reformed* was being used in ambiguous and confusing ways. He complains that when theologians as diverse as John Calvin and Friedrich Schleiermacher (sometimes called "the father of liberalism") are both described as "Reformed," the word has been emptied of any concrete meaning.

Equally striking contrasts of more recent vintage could be cited. For example, the greatest theologian of the twentieth century, Karl Barth, is often hailed as a "Reformed theologian." This is particularly so in Europe, where Anglican and Lutheran theologians usually regard Barth as distinctively Reformed. In fact, they often complain that Barth is too Reformed. But no one has opposed Barth more vigorously than Cornelius Van Til, the Orthodox Presbyterian theologian who taught apologetics for many years at Westminster Seminary. As far as Van Til is concerned, Karl Barth is one of the most dangerous enemies of the Reformed faith.

It is also noteworthy that the leaders of two diametrically opposed ecumenical organizations were "Reformed." The Dutch theologian, W.A. Visser 't Hooft, was the first president of the World Council of Churches. The American Bible Presbyterian churchman Carl McIntyre was formerly president of the now-splintered International Council of Christian Churches. McIntyre's goal was to destroy the World Council of Churches. He regarded its leader as an instrument of the devil.

1

Yet, as with Barth and Van Til, both Visser 't Hooft and McIntyre claimed to be representing the true Reformed tradition! Obviously, what Niesel wrote forty years ago is still true.

Consequently, it might appear foolhardy to attempt to explain within a few pages what the word *Reformed* really stands for. Therefore, a caveat. Although I shall be stating rather dogmatically how I understand this word, I readily recognize a pluralism of more or less authentic Reformed accents or positions within the various members of the Reformed family of churches. For example, within the Reformed Church in America alone it is possible to discern about ten different approaches to the Reformed faith, all of which have some claim to legitimacy.[2]

Although there is considerable latitude within this framework of the tradition, there is a definite and distinctive Reformed approach to the Christian faith. My purpose is to clarify that tradition, lest the word *Reformed* become an empty shibboleth, devoid of any substance or significance. This danger is not imaginary. It is exposed in a frank, hardhitting address by Dr. James I. McCord, President of Princeton Theological Seminary, given at Geneva Forum in 1976. Speaking to his own United Presbyterian Church, he bewails all of the new "pop-theologies" (death of God, secular theology, situation ethics) which hit the headlines in the 1960s. "We reached the point," he says, of "corporate theological amnesia." Then follows a devasting self-criticism: "We have forgotten, really, our theological heritage, and one of the great responsibilities of the Church today is to regain the heart and meaning of our tradition, namely, what our faith is, who we are, and whose we are."[3]

United Presbyterians are not the only ones who are in danger of losing their identity. Hence it is not only interesting but also urgent that those of us in the Reformed tradition reexamine our theological roots and review honestly our present state and future prospects.

I propose to do this by suggesting a number of misunderstandings, myths, and caricatures concerning the Reformed tradition (or Calvin, or Calvinism—none of which are quite the same). I am not fighting straw men or beating dead horses. I have personally encountered all of these misunderstandings either in fairly recent books, in ecumenical contexts in Europe, Japan, or the United States, or within my own denomination. In general, my criteria for evaluating and judging these misunderstandings are Calvin and the classical Reformed confessions of the sixteenth and seventeenth centuries, especially those in my own tradition.

In order to cover ground I shall have to be blunt, brief, and simple. This means that I shall occasionally indulge in generalizations which, ideally, would be hedged by all kinds of qualifications. In all of these misunderstandings or caricatures there is a germ of truth. Accordingly, the result of this study should be humbling as well as gratifying.

ONE

Misunderstanding One

*That the word "Reformed" refers primarily
to those denominations which bear that name,
especially those of Dutch origin.*

THIS MISUNDERSTANDING is largely limited to Americans who
have some contact with either the Reformed or Christian
Reformed Churches. However, I find that even many people
who belong to these Churches have little appreciation of the
scope of the Reformed tradition.

The term *Reformed* as a designation for a denomination or
family of churches is a late-Reformation development. In the
1560s, the word came to be used on the continent in a
somewhat official way, but it was almost an equivalent of
"Protestant" or "Evangelical" and included Lutherans as well
as those churches affiliated with Zwingli* or Calvin. It was
only after 1590 that a distinction came to be made between
Lutherans and Reformed.[1]

Reformed subsequently came to be used of almost all the
Calvinist churches on the continent—*Eglise Reformed* in
France, *Reformierte Kirche* in Germany and the German-
speaking part of Switzerland (often preceded by the word
Evangelische), *Hervormde* or *Gereformeerde Kerken* in the

---

*Zwingli was the first "Reformed" reformer. He began his efforts in Zurich,
Switzerland, only a few years after Luther began his in Germany. More information
follows.

5

Netherlands. The word implied "reformed according to the Word of God." The term "Presbyterian," on the other hand, refers primarily to a form of church order (derived from the Greek word *presbyterous* meaning presbyter or elder) and is used by Reformed Churches of Anglo-Saxon origin. Theologically, there are no significant differences between the two. John Knox, the founder of the Presbyterian Church in Scotland, was not only a close friend and disciple of Calvin's; he also faithfully represented Calvin's theological position.

The origins of the Reformed tradition are, by no means, in the Netherlands—nor in Scotland, where Presbyterianism, as such, developed. In the early and mid-sixteenth century in Europe many diverse streams flowed together to make up the Reformed tradition.

First, there was Ulrich Zwingli, a Swiss-German, who claimed that he "had begun to preach the gospel" (i.e., in an evangelical, Protestant manner) already in 1516, a year before Luther posted his ninety-five theses on the church door at Wittenberg. It was not until he became the preaching minister of the Grossmünster Church in Zurich in 1519, however, that he began to challenge the Roman Catholic Church in a more formal way. The Reformation movement in Zurich took place gradually between the years 1519 and 1523. The reform movement quickly spread to other parts of German-speaking Switzerland: to Basel under the leadership of Oecolampadius; to Bern under the leadership of Berthold Haller; and to St. Gallen, Schaffhausen, and Glarus under the leadership of lesser-known figures. Also between 1522 and 1532, the Reformed side of the Reformation spread to French-speaking centers in Switzerland such as Lausanne, under Viret; Neuchâtel; and Geneva, under Farel. Viret, Farel, and Calvin, who later was enlisted by Farel to assist him in Geneva, were all of French origin.

The reform movement in France—again quite distinct from the Lutheran movement in Germany—began to take shape in the 1530s. But, a decade earlier, Martin Bucer, of the Alsace district, spearheaded the Reformation in Strasbourg. In places as far away as Poland (under à Lasco) and Hungary (somewhat later), churches sympathetic to Calvin were coming into being. The Waldensians in Italy, whose history antedates the sixteenth-century Reformation, held a synod in 1532 in which they aligned themselves with the Reformed Churches. The most popular and enduring confessional contribution of the Reformed Churches—the *Heidelberg Catechism* (1563)—comes from the German Reformed Church.

It was not until the second half of the sixteenth century that the Scottish Presbyterian and Dutch Reformed Churches were organized. In fact, the first Protestants in the Netherlands were Lutherans. They were followed by Anabaptists and Mennonites. The Reformed element was only the third Protestant wave to enter the Netherlands!

In our own time, although the Reformed Churches in the Netherlands are particularly virile and influential, one should not equate the term *Reformed* with Dutch Churches. In the Netherlands itself all the Reformed Churches put together only constitute about forty percent of the total population. More important, the leading Protestant Churches in Switzerland, Hungary, and France are Reformed. Italy's Waldensian Church is basically Reformed in its theology. There are still significant Reformed Churches in Germany and Poland. When the Presbyterian Churches in Scotland, England, and Ireland are added, it is obvious that *Reformed* describes one of the largest families of churches in Europe. It is estimated that in the world today there are over twenty-five million Christians who consider themselves Reformed.

In the United States Reformed/Presbyterian Churches make up the third largest Protestant group. Some of the largest Protestant denominations in Asia, Africa, and Latin America are also of Reformed/Presbyterian background. The leading Protestant churches in Mexico, Brazil, Korea, Taiwan, and Indonesia (not to mention South Africa, which has given the name unwanted notoriety) are all Reformed/Presbyterian. The largest Reformed/Presbyterian congregations in the world today are no longer in traditional centers such as Geneva,

Amsterdam, Edinburgh, or Pittsburgh, but rather in Nairobi, Seoul, and Sao Paulo!

It should also be noted that in the United States and the British Commonwealth there are numerous ministers and theologians who serve Baptist, Congregational, and Anglican (Episcopalian) Churches but who consider themselves basically "Reformed" in their theology. I find it intriguing, for example, that for many years the standard text in systematic theology at Western Seminary was not that by the famous Presbyterian Charles Hodge or by Christian Reformed scholar Louis Berkhof, but the three-volume work of Augustus Hopkins Strong, a Baptist theologian from Rochester Seminary.[2] One of the leading Calvin scholars in the United States, the late Ford Lewis Battles, was of Congregational background,[3] and many of the finest Calvin scholars in the English-speaking world are Anglicans: Philip Hughes, James I. Packer, and T.H.L. Parker.

In conclusion, then, *Reformed* comprehends a large, international group of churches as well as countless individuals who belong to denominations that are called neither Reformed nor Presbyterian. Hence, any time we who belong to the Dutch Churches (RCA or CRC) here in the United States imagine that we are the principal representatives of the Reformed tradition, we are both presumptuous and in egregious error. On the other hand, there is no need to be shy or defensive about the name simply because in the Anglo-Saxon world the term *Presbyterian* is better known. Few ecclesiastical/theological terms are more respected and honored than that of *Reformed*.

We can be justly proud as long as we remember that the word denotes a task more than an accomplishment. *Ecclesia reformate semper reformanda est!* "A Reformed church must ever be reforming itself"[4]—in accordance with the Word of God.

TWO

Misunderstanding Two

*Since Reformed/Presbyterian Churches adhere to creeds
and confessions they are not biblical.*

THIS CRITICISM comes largely from Christians of Baptist and
free church (Congregational, Methodist, Holiness) backgrounds, particularly those of an independent, fundamentalist
style. Some simply assume that anyone who recites a creed or
acknowledges even the relative authority of a confession
thereby undercuts the true authority of the scriptures.[1]

As with most misunderstandings, there is, unfortunately,
some reason for the confusion. Earlier generations in Reformed/
Presbyterian Churches often tried to settle theological argu-
ments by citing some well-known phrase or statement from the
Heidelberg Catechism or the *Westminster Confession* (more rarely
the *Belgic Confession* or *Canons of Dort*). Today, our confessions
are not as well known and play little or no role in theological
discussions. They are now usually only appealed to when
someone has his back against the wall or is trying to down an
opponent. Even worse, our standards are occasionally cited by
those who have not even read them carefully or who use phrases
out of context.

The danger of an unbiblical confessionalism is always
present, but our confessions themselves give no warrant for it.
The *Genevan Confession* of 1536, for example, begins with the
words: "First we affirm that we desire to follow Scripture
alone as the rule of faith and religion, without mixing with it

any other thing which might be devised by the opinion of men apart from the Word of God, and without wishing to accept for our spiritual government any other doctrine than what is conveyed to us by the same Word without addition or diminution, according to the command of our Lord."[2] This is typical of the more detailed statements found in the subsequent confessions of the Swiss, French, Dutch, and Scottish Reformed Churches.[3]

The *Belgic Confession* (1561) similarly affirms that we may not "put on equal footing any writings of men, however holy they may have been, with the divine Scriptures; nor custom with the truth of God . . . , nor the great multitude; nor antiquity; nor the succession of times or persons; nor the councils, decrees or statutes [and, by implication, "nor the *Belgic Confession* or any other confession"]. . . . Therefore, we reject with our whole heart whatever does not agree with this infallible rule . . ." (Article 7).*

The *Westminster Confession,* a product of the Church of Scotland in the next century (1646), is equally emphatic in regard to this question. "The supreme judge, by which all controversies of religion are to be determined, and all decrees of councils, opinions of ancient writers, doctrines of men, and private spirits, are to be examined, and in whose sentence we are to rest, can be no other but the Holy Spirit speaking in Scripture" (Chapter I, Section X).

This stress on the unique authority and sole sufficiency of the Word of God is the foundation of the Reformed tradition. It is doubtful whether anyone who claims to be Reformed (or Lutheran) would ever admit to elevating a confession above the Word. But if, by inference or practice, we ever give the impression that this is the case, we are at that moment distinctly un-Reformed.[4]

In the history of the Church, however, confessionalism has

---

*These classic confessions have appeared in any number of editions: Cochrans' *Reformed Confessions* and John H. Leith, *Creeds of the Churches,* are only two. References to them will appear in parentheses in the text henceforth.

been a serious problem at times. For the Reformed Churches, generally, confessions have not played the role they have in Lutheranism;[5] nor have they assumed the authority of the dogmas of the Roman Catholic Church. Karl Barth had considerable experience of both of these other confessional groups and, early in his career, noted:

> The Reformed creeds differ from the Augsburg Confession and others by the fact that in committing themselves, at a measured distance, to the *one object* of all thought, they follow a course which, though less dramatic and effective for theology, at least saves them from staking everything upon the card of *any doctrine*. They refer all doctrine away from itself to the one Object. To them *truth* is God—not their *thought* about God but God *himself* and God *alone,* as he speaks his own *word* in Scripture and in Spirit.[6]

Barth's criticisms of Lutherans may no longer be valid in the United States except in one case. In its recent struggle, the Lutheran Church Missouri Synod has accorded ever greater authority to its collection of confessions, *The Book of Concord.* In the Reformed tradition there has never been one catechism or one confession, as in Lutheranism, but rather a wide variety of catechisms and confessions. Again, in contrast to Luther, Calvin's own catechisms have never had an authoritative place in any of the Reformed Churches outside of Geneva in the sixteenth century. Hence Arthur Cochrane may not be overstating the situation when he declares that "there is no such thing as a Reformed *corpus doctrinae* [body of doctrine]."[7]

This recognition of a wide variety of confessional standards in the various Reformed and Presbyterian Churches, while admirable in some respects, also has its drawbacks. Some churches, like the German-speaking Reformed Church in Switzerland, have no confessions. The United Presbyterian Church, U.S.A., since 1967, has had a *Book of Confessions* which contains nine statements ranging from the *Apostles' Creed* to the *Barmen*

Confession (German Evangelical Church, 1934) and their own *Confession of 1967.*

The advantage of such a collection is that their seventeenth-century Scottish standards—the *Westminster Catechisms* and *Westminster Confession*—have been immeasurably enriched by the addition of two classics, the *Heidelberg Catechism* (1563) and the *Second Helvetic* (i.e., Swiss) *Confession* (1566). (The former is generally regarded as the "jewel" of Reformation catechisms. Charles Hodge thought the latter "the most authoritative symbol of the Reformed Church." His judgment is shared by many modern historians.) The problem with such a large collection, especially in a denomination like the United Presbyterian Church, is the danger that none of them will be taken very seriously. At best, the more liberal types will opt for the *Confession of 1967*, whereas conservatives will cling to the *Westminster Confession* to the exclusion of the other riches in the whole collection.

A truly Reformed and reforming church must ever confess its faith anew. Problems and challenges are involved in this need for new confessions. New heresies and ideologies cannot be countered effectively by mouthing archaic and irrelevant battle cries. Most Calvinists, even of a conservative stripe, would acknowledge this in principle.[8] But when it comes to writing a new confession, invariably a wave of opposition rises, usually from the conservative wing in the church. The opposition is sometimes justifiable. Too many contemporary confessions tend to be one-sided and weak or fuzzy concerning certain key doctrinal issues. In far too many cases, however, one has the impression that the resistance is to change itself, even when the older, traditional confessions are no longer meaningful or relevant.

Recent (i.e., since World War II) attempts in the Reformed community of churches have met with only moderate success. In March 1946, the Netherlands Reformed Church appointed a committee to investigate the possibility of formulating a new doctrinal statement in order to meet the needs its members were feeling after the war. The result was *Foundations and Perspec-*

tives of Confession, adopted by their General Synod in 1950. A supplementary statement, *The Doctrine Concerning Holy Scripture,* was approved in 1954. Both were made available in English translation by the New Brunswick Seminary faculty in 1955.[9]

The point of departure is the kingdom of God, which is both a special Reformed theme and a very existential matter for people who had recently experienced foreign tyranny and idolatrous ideologies. Especially interesting (and *Dutch* Reformed) are the treatments of history, civil authority, and the election and future of Israel.

In the United States, there were at least three major attempts to compose new confessions in the 1960s. (The Reformed Church in America actually initiated proceedings in 1957.) The first to be approved was the *Confession of 1967* of the United Presbyterian Church, U.S.A. The overarching theme— reflective of the turmoil of the 1960s—was reconciliation. Unfortunately, the adoption of this confession turned out to be divisive, but this was probably to be expected in our pluralistic age.

The Southern Presbyterians also began working on a new confession in the 1960s and came out with *A Declaration of Faith* in 1972. As with the United Presbyterians, this confession was submitted as a part of a *Book of Confessions* to the denomination for approval in 1977. It failed to gain the necessary approval of three fourths of the presbyteries. The most serious objection was that, in seeking to please all the elements in the church, the new confession alienated both conservative and more liberal segments of the church.

The Reformed Church, which was the first to begin, was the last to accept its new confession, *Our Song of Hope,* at its General Synod of 1978. Even then it was not considered a confession on the level of the *Belgic Confession* or the *Canons of Dort* but "as a statement of the church's faith for use in its ministry of witness, teaching, and worship."[10] *Our Song* is unique among modern-day confessions in that it was not done by a committee but by an individual, Dr. Eugene Heiderman.

He was then Chairman of the Religion Department at Central College in Pella, Iowa, later academic dean at Western Seminary, and now Secretary for World Missions, RCA.[11] (An earlier attempt in 1966 by the Theological Commission had not met with much enthusiasm.) This accounts for the creativity and consistency of *Our Song*. Though thoroughly contemporary, it also reflects at several key points the influence of A.A. van Ruler, Heideman's mentor during his graduate study at the University of Utrecht.

This confession has won more general acceptance than most recent attempts, but the response is still disappointing. The majority of Reformed/Presbyterian Christians today, whatever their theological orientation, do not seem to appreciate the significance and possibilities of creeds and confessions for personal faith and corporate church life.[12]

In response to all these concerns, therefore, I would like to point out why confessions are important and necessary—and biblical. The Bible itself is a confessional book. Romans 10:9f. is the most obvious text in this regard, but there are countless passages which allude to the necessity of the corollaries of faith and confession (1 Cor 12:3; 1 Tm 6:13; 1 Jn 4:2).[13] The ancient maxim is "I believe; therefore I confess." As M.E. Osterhaven pointedly comments, "An unconfessed faith is a dead faith. Where faith is real there is confession."[14]

It is a myth to imagine that one can have Christ without confessions, the scriptures without credal formulations. Even Baptists, Pentecostals, independent fundamentalists, and free-thinking liberals have their credal formulas or statements, whether they acknowledge them as such or not. The Bible is simply too big and complex a book to provide the individual believer or the church with meaningful guidelines without some clue to its interpretation.[15] This, in effect, is what a creed or confession does.

The purpose of creeds and confessions is not to condemn or cut off those with whom we differ but rather to unite and strengthen. In the history of the church, creeds have been misused. They have been imposed on others and have shackled freedom of investigation. Paul Woolley is quite right when he reminds us that their "primary purpose is educational and evangelistic." They should be "joyful, happy proclamations of the great freedom that is true Christian living."[16]

This is why it has been said, "Creeds should be sung, not debated!"

THREE

Misunderstanding Three

*That Reformed Churches are only those with
a Presbyterian church order.*

THE WORD *Reformed* refers primarily to a theological tradition, not a system of church government or polity. Even so, most Reformed Churches have had a presbyterian system of government throughout their respective histories. However, there are many variations within what is considered a presbyterian system of church government. For example, deacons have not played as prominent a role in American Presbyterian as in American Reformed Churches.[1] In the Christian Reformed Church the General Synod has more legislative power than in the Reformed Church in America, where the classes (presbyteries) have more authority. Also, the Reformed Church in America is the only denomination which still maintains the fourth office—that of professor or doctor of theology—first instituted by Calvin in Geneva.[2]

Calvin and his spiritual heirs have always considered church order or polity to be very important.[3] They have even maintained that the presbyterian system of church government was the one closest to scripture. But at the same time, they have always allowed for considerable diversity and have never advocated a slavish following of the early church.[4] John Leith expresses well these two truths when he says, on the one hand, that Presbyterians take "polity seriously because of its significance for theology. Faith cannot be separated from form,"

17

whereas on the other hand, "Reformed theology has never made the existence of the church dependent on polity."[5]

What really matters, in the last analysis, is not whether there are bishops or not, two offices (ministers and elders) or four offices (ministers, elders, deacons, and professors of theology), but whether Christ is truly Lord of his church.[6] As the great Calvin scholar Emile Doumergue rightly points out, for Calvin "the headship of Christ is not only spiritual and moral, it has to do with [church] polity and law."[7] This lordship of Christ in turn depends on whether Christ is faithfully proclaimed and present in word and sacrament and whether his honor maintained through church discipline.

The key to the presbyterian system of government is the *elder* or *presbyter*. It is not exaggerating to say that "the office is of such importance to the polity of the Reformed [or Presbyterian] Church that without it the church would lose its character as a Reformed Church."[8] Although this pattern of church government stems from Calvin (who, in turn, was much indebted to the Strasbourg reformer, Martin Bucer), the elders in the Genevan Church hardly resembled the elders or presbyters of the New Testament churches, nor did they function in many ways like our elders.[9] Together with the ministers, they were responsible for church discipline and the care of souls. But unlike elders or presbyters of a later age, the Genevan elders were not elected by the congregation. Rather, they were chosen from and elected by the city councils, a concession wrung from Calvin by the Genevan magistrates.

Another fundamental principle in presbyterian polity is that of the *parity of the ministry*. Calvin was remarkably tolerant of the titles and forms of ecclesiastical office, but he was opposed to any hierarchical notions. This spirit finds expression in most of the Reformed confessions, including the *Belgic Confession*: "As for ministers of the Word, they have, wherever they are, the same power and authority, being one and all, servants of Jesus Christ, the one universal Bishop and only Head of the Church" (Article 31).

Calvin did not object to bishops—as long as the fundamental

parity of ministry was acknowledged. Some eminent Calvin scholars like John T. McNeill and John Leith maintain that Calvin approved, even if he did not advocate, episcopacy. "In actual practice Calvin accepted the episcopal system where it existed as long as it was purged of the trappings of imperial status and tyranny and so long as bishops were active in preaching, teaching, and pastoral care."[10] Proof of this is found not only in Calvin's tolerance of bishops in the Reformed Churches in Poland and Hungary but also in his cordial relationship (through correspondence) with Archbishop Cranmer of the Church of England.

In Scotland, however, there soon developed a strong animus toward the episcopacy on the part of Presbyterians. However, it was Andrew Melville,* not John Knox, who was absolutely opposed to bishops and an episcopal system. Later Puritans also strongly resisted episcopacy in any form.[11]

It is still debated today among Reformed and Presbyterian scholars whether a presbyterian order is essential to a Reformed Church. Even a doughty Reformed theologian like Wilhelm Niesel does not insist upon a particular set of offices in a Reformed Church.[12] Generally, however, the presbyterian system of church government best expresses Reformed theological convictions about the nature of the church.

This does not mean that one cannot be Reformed and belong to a denomination whose polity is congregational or episcopal. In fact, some of the less fortunate elements of both of those other systems are very much with the Reformed even though we prefer not to admit it! Some of our ministers and leaders act like Roman priests and bishops. Some of our churches are extremely congregational in their practice. Nevertheless, I concur with G.D. Henderson when he concludes that while

no ecclesiastical pattern of government will be faultless or equal to all spiritual circumstances, . . . the Presbyterian

---

*Melville was a Scottish reformer who was influenced by Calvin's successor in Geneva, Beza. He returned to Scotland in 1574, two years after the death of Knox, and became the leader of the Scottish Presbyterians.

scheme as a whole has stood the test of efficiency . . . and has proved acceptable and potent for centuries against numerous races and types. . . . This form of government has not only the encouragement of Bible support, but has been associated with helpful doctrine as to the sovereignty of God and the Headship of Christ and the activity of the Holy Spirit; recognition of the need for personal faith, response, individuality, as against externalism and superstition; emphasis on the divine calling of the laity; ethical stress represented by the doctrine of sanctification; zeal for spiritual independence; distaste for superiority; readiness for intercommunion; insistence upon the priority of the Word.[13]

In short, the best church polity is that which best glorifies Christ, edifies his people, and equips and frees them for witness and service in the world. To the extent that the presbyterian order does that, it helps the church to be truly Reformed according to the Word of God.

FOUR

Misunderstanding Four

*That Reformed/Presbyterian Churches are "low"
church and hence nonliturgical.*

MANY PEOPLE are probably not even aware of the fact that
churches are generally categorized as "high" or "low," depend-
ing on the degree to which they use a formal liturgy. Further,
liturgy, unfortunately, is often conceived of as ritual and
trappings—such as ministers wearing robes or vestments,
candles, an altar instead of a table, and choral amens. All of
these have little or nothing to do with liturgy as such. Liturgy,
most simply defined, is a church's "mode of worship."[1] The
word "liturgy" is a biblical term which refers broadly to the
public service of God, as well as to more specific acts of priestly
service. See 2 Corinthians 9:12 and Philippians 2:30, and then
Luke 1:23 and Hebrews 8:6 (translated as "ministry" in both
KJV and RSV, with exception of Lk 1:23 in KJV) and 9:21
(translated "ministry," "worship" [RSV], "ceremonies"
[NIV], and "divine service" [NEB]).

Every church has a liturgy, i.e., a form and order of worship,
even if it is not found in any liturgical book. Reformed
Churches have always had fully defined, complete orders of
worship. From the liturgies of Strasbourg (1540-1545) and
Geneva (1542) of Calvin's day, to the *Liturgy of the Reformed
Church in the Palatinate,* which was a companion piece to the
Heidelberg Catechism (1563), and the *Westminster Directory*
(1644) of the Scottish Presbyterian Church.[2] Hence, this

21

particular misunderstanding is a curious one—particularly on the part of our ministers. We have always had a liturgy. The only nonliturgical Reformed Church I know of is the German-speaking branch of the Swiss Reformed Church. Even they, in their own way, have a set, albeit very simple and plain, form of worship.

When I was a student, I recall hearing on occasion that we were a semi-liturgical church. I presumed that the "semi" meant that we somewhere between Episcopalians and Lutherans, on the one hand, and Baptists and Holiness Churches, on the other. As far as I can determine, the "semi" refers only to the fact that we allow for free prayers during our regular Sunday services, although not when we celebrate the sacraments according to prescribed forms. Another explanation is found in a little brochure, *RCA? Never Heard of It!* published by the Office of Promotion and Communications of the Reformed Church in America: "Our worship is 'semi-liturgical,' which simply means that we are somewhere between very formal and very informal."

On the occasion of the one-hundredth anniversary of Western Seminary, Dr. Howard Hageman gave a series of lectures on the history of Reformed Church liturgies and documented the sad fortunes of Reformed liturgics.[3] Even before our forefathers came to these shores in 1628, the liturgies in use in most Reformed Churches had been undermined to some extent by Zwingli's influence, who had a lower view of the sacraments than either Calvin or Knox. The liturgical history of the Reformed Churches has, at least until recently, been spotty. But since World War II, Reformed Churches, both European and American, have been in the forefront of liturgical renewal.[4] Renewal does not mean adding high church refinements like vestments or candles, but returning to Reformation roots and above all to the biblical character of worship.

In my own particular tradition a major breakthrough in this regard was the adoption in 1968 of a new *Liturgy and Psalms,*[5] a great improvement over its predecessor of 1906. This new liturgy has its weaknesses, but it is generally regarded as an outstanding contribution to the worship and praise of God. It also represents a significant recovery of many of Calvin's insights.

Not the least of its virtues is the order for the sacrament of the Lord's Supper. The sacrament is explained in terms of the past, present, and future aspects of communion with our Lord: It is "a feast of remembrance, of communion, and of hope."[6] The language used to describe the nature of our participation in Christ is significant. Our Lord "makes himself known to us as the true heavenly Bread that strengthens us unto life eternal" and as "the Vine in whom we must abide if we are to bear fruit."[7] When we partake of the bread and the wine he "as certainly feeds and nourishes our hungry and thirsty souls with his crucified body and shed blood to everlasting life, as this bread is broken before your eyes and this cup is given to you . . ."[8]

Note that here we have a *real presence* and a *real partaking* of Jesus Christ. The bread and the wine are not mere symbols of the broken body and shed blood of Christ. By faith, and through the operation of the Holy Spirit, we spiritually partake of Jesus Christ. *Spiritual* in this case does not mean symbolical or unreal. As the *Second Helvetic Confession* points out, "By spiritual food we do not mean some sort of imaginary food, but the very body of the Lord given to us, which nevertheless is received by the faithful, not corporeally, but spiritually by faith" (Article XXI).[9] All of the Reformers, except Zwingli, had a high view of the sacrament.[10] Ironically, it is the view of Zwingli, rather than that of Calvin or Knox, which is the common understanding of the sacrament in most Reformed/ Presbyterian Churches.

Calvin's view of what takes place in the celebration of the Lord's Supper is even more realistic than that expressed in the *Liturgy*. Especially graphic is his description in one passage:

> To summarize: Our souls are fed by the flesh and blood of Christ in the same way that bread and wine keep and sustain physical life. For the analogy of the sign applies only if souls

find their nourishment in Christ—which cannot happen unless Christ truly grows into one with us, and refreshes us by the eating of his flesh and the drinking of his blood.

Even though it seems unbelievable that Christ's flesh, separated from us by such great distance, penetrates to us, so that it becomes our food, let us remember how far the secret power of the Holy Spirit towers above all our senses, and how foolish it is to wish to measure his immeasurableness by our measure. What, then, our mind does not comprehend, let faith conceive: that the Spirit truly unites things separate in space.

Now, that sacred partaking of his flesh and blood, by which Christ pours his life into us, as if it penetrated into our bones and marrow, he also testifies and seals in the Supper—not by presenting a vain and empty sign, but by manifesting there the effectiveness of his Spirit to fulfill what he promises. And truly he offers and shows the reality there signified to all who sit at that spiritual banquet, although it is received with benefit by believers alone, who accept such great generosity with true faith and gratefulness of heart.*

An anomaly in this connection is the infrequency with which we usually celebrate the Lord's Supper. It is ironic, because Calvin himself wanted to have the sacrament celebrated in Geneva every Lord's Day (IV.17.43). He was thwarted by the City Council whose thinking was still largely libertine and influenced by Roman Catholic tradition.[12] It was they who insisted it could only be celebrated four times a year. So in this regard we are the heirs of Calvin's opponents rather than Calvin himself. (Weekly celebration might never be feasible in most of our churches, but the approach of many Japanese churches, viz., a monthly celebration, might be a happy compromise.)

The distinctiveness of Reformed worship, however, does not

---

*This is from Calvin's *Institutes of the Christian Religion*, IV.17.10. Such references will be henceforth incorporated into the text so: (IV.17.10). The *Institutes* are available in a number of editions.[11] For Calvin, here as elsewhere, the key is the Holy Spirit. "The Sacraments profit not a whit without the power of the Holy Spirit" (IV.14.9).

lie so much in its sacramental teaching or practice as in its emphasis on biblical preaching and in its great musical heritage, the metrical psalm.

The Reformation was in many ways simply a restoration of preaching. The Swiss Reformation began when Zwingli came to the Grossmünster (Great Cathedral) in Zurich, opened his Greek text and began preaching straight through the Gospel of Matthew—a revolutionary practice in that time. When Calvin came to Geneva to bring order out of chaos in that recently reformed church, he did many things: wrote a confession, a catechism, and a new church order. He was also busy administering, writing countless letters and tracts, and giving lectures on the Bible. But above all, he preached: Monday, Wednesday, Friday, and twice on Sunday. At one point, he preached every week day in alternate weeks until this became too tiring.[13] Calvin, the theologian par excellence, was first of all a preacher.

For Calvin, to reject or despise the preaching of the Word "is like blotting out the face of God which shines upon us" in such preaching.

> For among the many excellent gifts with which God has adorned the human race, it is a singular privilege that he deigns to consecrate to himself the mouths and tongues of men in order that his voice may resound in them. Let us accordingly not in turn dislike to embrace obediently the doctrine of salvation put forth by his command and by his own mouth. For although God's power is not bound to outward means, he has nonetheless bound us to this ordinary manner of teaching. Fanatical men, refusing to hold fast to it, entangle themselves in many deadly snares. Many are led either by pride, dislike, or rivalry to the conviction that they can profit enough from private reading and meditation; hence they despise public assemblies and deem preaching superfluous. But, since they do their utmost to sever or break the sacred bond of unity, no one escapes the just penalty of this unholy separation without bewitching himself with pestilent errors and foulest delusions. In order, then, that

pure simplicity of faith may flourish among us, let us not be reluctant to use this exercise of religion which God, by ordaining it, has shown us to be necessary and highly approved. (IV.1.5)

This exalted view of preaching finds its most eloquent expression in the highly regarded *Second Helvetic Confession* of 1566 where it is boldly stated: The preaching of the Word of God is the Word of God.[14] Then follows this explanation (Chapter I):

Wherefore when this Word of God is now preached in the church by preachers lawfully called, we believe that the very word of God is proclaimed, and received by the faithful; and that neither any other Word of God is to be invented nor is to be expected from heaven: and that now the Word itself which is preached is to be regarded, not the minister that preaches; for even if he be evil and a sinner, nevertheless the Word of God remains still true and good.

Fortunately, this aspect of the Reformed tradition has been preserved with surprising fidelity. To this day, biblical preaching has been one of the strengths of Reformed worship although the number of Reformed/Presbyterian pulpits where solid expository preaching is heard is, unfortunately, in decline. It may be one of the most significant contributions of the Reformed tradition to the ecumenical movement.[15]

The same fidelity cannot be claimed for that other distinctive contribution of Reformed worship—the metrical psalm. Traditionally, preaching and psalm singing were the hallmarks of Reformed worship. In the modern era, this rich heritage has been sold for a mess of pop-pottage, especially in more conservative Reformed/Presbyterian Churches.

Among the treasures Calvin bequeathed to his heirs were not only the *Institutes of the Christian Religion,* his commentaries and sermons, catechisms and church order, but also the *Genevan Psalter* (which was completed by Calvin's colleague and successor, Theodore Beza, in 1562). For three centuries this psalter was *the* hymnbook for most of the Protestant churches in Switzerland, France, the Netherlands, England, Scotland, and the United States.

The metrical psalm and psalm paraphrases have dominated the hymnals of Scotland and the Netherlands up to the present. In the United States, metrical psalms almost disappeared from most Presbyterian-Reformed hymnals in the latter part of the nineteenth century and first half of the twentieth century. *The Hymnbook*, published by the Reformed Church in America along with a number of Presbyterian denominations in 1955, was a marked improvement over the hymnals being then used in many Midwestern RCA congregations. *The Hymnbook* has seventy-five psalms or psalm paraphrases in contrast to forty-three in the older Presbyterian hymnal and an even smaller number in the gospel hymnals used in many of our churches.[16] It was left to the Christian Reformed,[17] Orthodox Presbyterian,[18] and Covenanter denominations to preserve this heritage. In the first half of our century, most mainline Presbyterian/Reformed denominations sold out to a hymnody that represented either the ornate, subjective, and often liberal spirit of the nineteenth century, or the individualistic, Arminian* flavor of the American revivals of roughly the same period. In the latter case the music was of an inferior quality.

The test of a good hymnal is not simply how many psalms it contains. The basic concerns of Calvin and his colleagues were also that the hymns used in corporate worship be scriptural, magnify God (rather than our experience), and be of the highest literary and musical quality. Therefore, Calvin acquired the help of Clement Marot, a poet, and Louis Bourgeois, a musician, for his *Genevan Psalter*. They were the finest France

---

*Arminius was a Dutch theologian (1560-1609) who challenged some of the teachings of traditional Calvinism, particularly those relating to predestination. He affirmed, for example, that grace is not irresistible and that Christians can fall from grace. His followers, known as Remonstrants or Arminians, were condemned as heretical at the famous Synod of Dort in 1618-1619 which came up with five counter-theses known as the five points of Calvinism (TULIP). Arminianism later became a hallmark of Methodism.

had to offer. Thus, in many ways, the decline of the psalter in Reformed hymnody is a sign of the secularization of our worship. The hymns that were used increasingly from the end of the nineteenth century onward were designed more to stir our emotions than glorify God. Their real purpose was entertainment not worship. Karl Barth put his finger on the problem when he wrote, "The secularisation of Protestantism, in the specific form of modernistic Neo-Protestantism, is only a symptom of the inner secularisation visible in the evolution of the hymn. . . . In every section of our hymnbooks we can find the hidden heresy involved in the whole development."[19]

Barth here is primarily describing the situation in Europe, but one need not look far to find not only "hidden heresies," but overt heresy, in many of our American hymnals. The situation has improved in most of the recent denominational hymnals, although it is debatable whether the fairly recent United Presbyterian *Worshipbook* (1972) is a significant advance over *The Hymnbook*. The same cannot be said for most of the recent interdenominational, popular hymnals[20] with the exception of *Hymns for the Living Church* (1974),[21] which is a marked improvement over its predecessor, *The Service Hymnal,* and its successor, *The Worship and Service Hymnal* (1957), which have been the most popular hymnals in Midwestern RCA churches for the last twenty-five years.

Why is it that *The Hymnbook* was resisted and rejected in the majority of Midwestern and Western RCA Churches? Not, it would appear, because there were a few liberal remnants in it (see, e.g., No. 512, stanza 4; No. 490, Stanza 1; No. 474 and 485), but rather because it did not include some of the old favorites, some of which were not included for good reason! Why not then the Christian Reformed *Psalter Hymnal* (1959; revised edition, 1976) or the Orthodox Presbyterian *Trinity Hymnal*? The answer is that distinctly Reformed hymnody has become alien and unpalatable to the majority of Reformed Church people. Their musical and theological tastes have become so dull and jaded that they prefer "In the Garden" and "Beulah Land" to Luther's "A Mighty Fortress" and Calvin's

"I Greet Thee, Who My Sure Redeemer Art."

What is objectionable about so many so-called gospel hymns is not only the cheap, jazzy music, but also the self-centered, Arminian theology. If it is true that sacred music "gives wings to theology" (Helen Dickinson), then it is time that we let our theology rather than our feelings determine our choice of hymnals, unless we no longer pretend to be Reformed.

It is not that proper Reformed hymnody should be heavy and musically sophisticated. Singing in church should be inspiring and uplifting. Moreover, there is a place for hymns which give expression to personal experience and piety. A marvelous example is Isaac Watts's "When I Survey the Wondrous Cross." It is basically a matter of balance. You need not be a theologian to figure out when there is an unhealthy imbalance. Simply notice whether you sing more hymns about "me and my salvation" or hymns about God, his glory and grace, and his kingdom. In many of the best hymns it is not a question of either/or, for both elements are present. Take, for example, "Jesus Thou Joy of Loving Hearts" or "How Firm a Foundation."

The problem in the Reformed Church in America is that we enjoy too much freedom when it comes to liturgy and worship. When one moves from pulpit to pulpit in our denomination—as I do—it is disconcerting, to say the least, to find every conceivable type of hymnal in the pews (including a *Country and Western Hymnal!*) and a frightful hodgepodge of orders of worship. How different it is in the Christian Reformed Church where there is one liturgy (which is followed) and one hymnal—although even there one finds secularizing inroads.

A leading Dutch liturgical scholar, G. van der Leeuw, once said, "Whoever takes the little finger of liturgy soons discovers that he has grabbed the whole fist of theology."[22] Our liturgy, or our lack thereof, determines how we worship. Our worship, more than anything else, determines our faith and piety. This is why the way we worship is so crucial. Here, far more than in the Sunday school or catechism class, our real theology is formed and nurtured. The situation in most Presbyterian/Reformed churches has improved in this regard in the last twenty-five years, but James I. McCord, President of Princeton Theological Seminary, may not be too pessimistic when he writes, "The malaise of the church is clearly seen in the impoverished worship of our congregations. Many of our churches are in this respect more 'deformed' than 'reformed.' "[23]

FIVE

Misunderstanding Five

*That Reformed theology is rationalistic
and scholastic in its approach.*

WITH THIS "MISUNDERSTANDING" we move from the historical
and ecclesiological realms to the more specifically doctrinal and
theological issues. It might be too difficult and abstract a topic
to bother with in a book of this sort. It is a rather technical and
complicated matter, but it is by no means irrelevant to our daily
faith and life. For the way we do theology—and all thinking
Christians theologize in one way or another—affects not only
the way in which we think about God, Christ, and our salvation,
but also shapes our attitudes, piety, and life-style. There is a
direct relation between arid, abstract, and doctrinaire theology,
and cold, lifeless, and negative Christianity.

The word scholasticism is often applied as a catchall to any
theological approach where there is little life or warmth and
where the mysteries and paradoxes of faith and existence are
reduced to neat, logical syllogisms.[1] Hence when the word
scholastic describes a theology, it is usually the kiss of death. The
great Swiss-American historian, Philip Schaff, describes
rationalism as one of "the diseases of Protestantism," because
like the scholastic theology of the Middle Ages, it tends to
degenerate into "dry dogmatism and stiffened orthodoxy"
where the doctrine of justification is separated abstractly from
holiness, and faith consists merely in sound doctrine divorced
from practical Christianity.[2]

31

Originally the term, however, referred to a tradition of philosophical and theological study and teaching in the Middle Ages. Thomas Aquinas (1224-1274), the greatest Roman Catholic systematic theologian of all time, revolutionized the theology of his time by using Aristotelian philosophy as the base for his new approach.[3] His *Summa Theologica* is regarded as the crowning achievement of scholastic theology. His method, in short, was to present a doctrine in argument, counterargument, and solution, using both faith and reason to demonstrate its coherence and truth. Here we have an early form of the dialectical method.[4] In the later medieval period (1300-1450), when theologians began to refine and elaborate the systems of earlier thinkers, this approach was occasionally labeled scholastic and the term came to have a pejorative meaning. For example, it was during this period that theologians allegedly had nothing better to do than debate about how many angels could dance on a pinhead!

By the time of Calvin, the scholastic approach had become arid and had fallen into disfavor. The reformers—especially Luther—spoke disparagingly of it and rejected the whole method. *Schoolmen* was a nasty word in Calvin's vocabulary. His references to Catholic theologians like Lombard (d. 1160) are nearly all in this vein.[5] Soon after Calvin's death, however, there developed a Protestant scholasticism. In fact, one only has to compare Calvin's treatment of predestination in the *Institutes* with the treatment of the same subject by his colleague and successor, Theodore Beza, to see the beginnings of Reformed scholasticism.[6] This came to full bloom in the seventeenth century—when the leading Lutheran and Reformed theologians used the Thomistic-Aristotelian approach in developing, refining, and, to some extent, deadening the dynamic theology of the sixteenth-century reformers.

We should not be too hard on those great seventeenth-century theologians. There were Reformed men like Johannes Wollebius, Gisbert Voetius, and Francis Turretin.[7] There were also Lutherans like Johann Gerhard, J.A. Quenstedt, and David Hollaz. They represent some brilliant theological scholarship. Their "school" has become generally known as Protestant Orthodoxy.[8]

But for all of its virtues, this side of theological thinking has also produced some unfortunate by-products. All theological systems rely to some extent on philosophical foundations. Augustine rested on Plato, Aquinas on Aristotle, Luther on Ockham, Calvin on Scotus. In our day Brunner draws on Kierkegaard, Barth on Kant and Hegel, and Tillich on Schelling.[9] The question to be asked in each case is the extent to which the resultant theology is faithful to the message and spirit of the Bible. In the case of the Protestant scholastics, it is increasingly felt that they unwittingly depended too much on neo-Aristotelian, Thomistic presuppositions which affected not only their method but also their message. The living faith of the reformers is gradually replaced by an increasing reliance on reason, and ever subtler distinctions and speculation. The net result is a static, rigid dogmatism and a dead orthodoxy. Despite all protestations to the contrary, in effect, scripture and faith are replaced by reason and logic.

What does all this—Aristotle, Aquinas, and seventeenth-century Protestant scholasticism—have to do with us today? Much in every way. As Heine, a nineteenth-century German novelist once said, "Nicht alles tot, was begraben ist" (Not everything is dead which has been buried).[10] There are some fascinating and curious connections between Turretin (the seventeenth-century Reformed theologian) and Charles Hodge (1797-1878) and Louis Berkhof (1873-1957) who produced systematic theologies which have made an indelible impact on several generations of American Presbyterian and Reformed ministers.[11] Moreover, in the case of Hodge, there is also the strong influence of an eighteenth-century philosophy called Scottish Realism.[12] According to H. Evan Runner, emeritus professor of philosophy at Calvin College, this movement has "had a devastating influence upon American Presbyterian circles." Runner cites the eminent American church historian Sydney Ahlstrom to show how "the foundation of Hodge's ethic and his conception of natural theology are Scottish rather than Calvinistic." Further, "Scottish Realism accelerated the long trend toward rational theology.... Reformed theology was thus emptied of its most dynamic element. A kind of rationalistic *rigor mortis* [literally, the stiffness of death] set in."[13]

More recently, Jack B. Rogers and Donald McKim, relying on the researches of John W. Stewart, have also pointed out how Scottish Realism, as well as Reformed scholasticism, have influenced Hodge and his contemporary disciples. Among them are John Gerstner and R.C. Sproul, the latter the director of the Ligonier Center near Pittsburgh. This has grave consequences for the whole inerrancy question and the "battle for the Bible."[14] Their thesis is that those who have been largely influenced by Turretin (and in the case of Hodge, Warfield, and their disciples also by Scottish Realism) have forsaken Calvin and our Reformation heritage for an alien approach to the Bible and the Christian faith.

Contemporary apologists as diverse as the late Edward John Carnell, Cornelius Van Til, Gordon Clark, and Francis Schaeffer on the one hand, and Carl Henry, Clark Pinnock, Harold Lindsell, and John Warwick Montgomery on the other are united in their reliance on reason and logic. Most, if not all of them, would probably concur with Moise Amyraut (1596-1664), a French theologian condemned as a liberal by most of his Reformed contemporaries, who wrote: "Belief in scriptural truths must be founded on reason and be consistent with proper logic."[15]

Manifest evidence of this is seen in Carl Henry's recent five-volume work, *God, Revelation and Authority,*[16] hailed as "the most important work of evangelical theology in modern times."[17] In a discussion of the method and criteria of theology, he baldly states that "theological verification is not dependent upon personal faith. ... If a person must first be a Christian believer in order to grasp the truth of revelation, then meaning is subjective and incommunicable."[18] Later, he makes similar claims: "In the theistic view, language is possible because of man's God-given endowment of rationality, of a-priori categories and of innate ideas. . . ." In short, what Henry holds out for is "a logically consistent divine revelation."[19] No wonder that Donald Bloesch complains about "the bent toward rationalism in current evangelicalism" as exemplified in theologians like Henry, Montgomery, Schaeffer, and Norman Geisler (of Dallas Theological Seminary).[20] He also points out that "in the tradition emanating from Protestant scholastic orthodoxy and the [old] Princeton School of theology . . . a high confidence is placed in the capacity of reason to judge the truth of revelation."[21]

Calvin would have been shocked to see the confidence in natural reason and logic which has become a hallmark of certain types of modern evangelicalism. No one has ever accused Calvin of being an irrationalist but at the same time he was very aware of the limits of our understanding. Man is "a rational being, differing from brute beasts," he avers, but then he quickly adds that "this light is choked with dense ignorance so that it cannot come forth effectively." Also, although reason "is a natural gift," it is so "weakened" and "corrupted" that only "misshapen ruins appear" (*Institutes*, II.2.12). Moreover, when it comes to "what human reason can discern with regard to God's kingdom and spiritual insight," the "greatest geniuses are blinder than moles!" (II.2.18).

What a contrast to the claims for reason in a theologian like Carl Henry! Where Clark, Henry, Lindsell, et al. appeal to reason and logic, Calvin appeals to God's grace and the gift of the Holy Spirit. Appealing to John 1:4-5 he comments, "This means: flesh is not capable of such lofty wisdom as to conceive God and what is God's, unless it be illumined by the Spirit of God" (II.2.19). This is something which "our Heavenly Father bestows on his elect through the Spirit of regeneration" (II.2.20). Contrary to our contemporary theological rationalists, Calvin steadfastly maintains that "man's mind can become spiritually wise only insofar as God illumines it" (II.2.20).

But what about the all-too-common portrayal of Calvin as an inflexible rationalist and legalist whose theology reflected a harsh, cold personality. This caricature is believed even by many Calvinists who have never read Calvin carefully. As John T. McNeill points out in his introduction to Calvin's *Institutes*:

> One who takes up Calvin's masterpiece with the preconception that its author's mind is a kind of efficient factory turning out and assembling the parts of a neatly jointed structure of dogmatic logic will quickly find this assumption challenged and shattered. The discerning reader soon realizes that not the author's intellect alone but his whole spiritual and emotional being is enlisted in his work. . . . He was not, we may say, a theologian by profession, but a deeply religious man who possessed a genius for orderly thinking and obeyed the impulse to write out the implications of his faith. He calls his book not a *summa theologiae* but a *summa pietatis*. The secret of his mental energy lies in his piety; its product is his theology, which is his piety described at length. His task is to expound (in the language of his original title) "the whole sum of piety and whatever it is necessary to know in the doctrine of salvation."[22]

A discriminating reading of the *Institutes* will bear out the truth of McNeill's contention. Calvin was not the legalistic logic-chopper and rationalistic dogmatician he is often portrayed to be. Compare the *Institutes* with most standard systematic theologies and it will become quite apparent how different Calvin's approach is. On the one hand, his theology is often suffused with a warm piety and evangelical passion which is often missing in orthodox theology texts.[23] On the other, there are some surprising gaps in the *Institutes* which make it far less logical and systematic than most dogmatic works.[24] The distinguished French Calvin scholar, Jean-Daniel Benoit, speaks of the *Institutes* as a work which has a decided appeal to the intelligence. "But what," he asks, "does this work have to do with the heart, the needs of souls, with that holy service which consists of the tact and concern required for spiritual guidance?

And yet, the *Institutes* is a religious book, in a certain respect, a book of piety perhaps more than a dogmatic treatise. It has nourished the spiritual life of many generations whose taste has not been dulled by daintiness and who were not afraid of strong nurture. . . . The *Institutes* is not only the book of a theologian; it is the book of a man who even before he became a pastor was haunted by a concern for souls."[25]

The *Heidelberg Catechism* (1563) breathes a spirit quite different from that of the *Westminster Catechism* written a century later (1648). The *Heidelberg Catechism* is noted for its experiential, practical approach to the faith. It does not begin with a theological prologue but a personal question about our only comfort in life and death. Throughout the catechism, after a doctrine is explained, the next focus frequently is: "What benefit do you receive?" Here is systematic theology which is, at the same time, eminently practical, pastoral theology.[26]

This combination of faith and learning, profound piety and a disciplined mind, is also found in several, more recent Reformed theologians. Within the Dutch Reformed tradition, one could cite names like Herman Bavinck[27] of a past generation, and contemporary theologians such as G.C. Berkouwer[28] and Hendrikus Berkhof.[29]

Reformed theology at its best is neither rationalistic nor scholastic, but a reverent witness of faith. As the famous Scottish theologian, T.F. Torrance, has written of Calvin, "Theology is fundamentally an act of worship."[30]

In conclusion, the way we do theology and think about our faith does have serious implications for our personal faith and our congregational life. Unfortunately, whether of Scottish Presbyterian or Dutch Reformed background, we are too often cool, if not cold, and reserved about our faith, and reluctant or unable to share it effectively. Traditionally, ours has been a head, not a heart, religion. Some of this may be due to our ethnic backgrounds and sub-cultures. But some of this approach to life and faith is due to a rationalistic, scholastic approach to theology. Admittedly, this is difficult to demonstrate. What is indisputable is that in certain conservative

Reformed/Presbyterian circles the heritage of Protestant scholasticism and Scottish Realism is a divisive and destructive force, more theological than scriptural.

There is a third way between theological laxity and rationalistic orthodoxy. Theologians like Bavinck and Berkouwer are thoroughly scholarly and scientific in their theologizing, yet bow humbly before the mysteries of the faith and the dynamic variety within God's Word. The result is first-class theology combined with reverence and praise. This kind of balance should be characteristic of all of us: always "prepared to make a defense to anyone who calls [us] to account for the hope that is in [us] . . ." but "with gentleness and reverence" (1 Pt 3:15). There is a balance between cool heads and warm hearts, between learning and piety.

Here again I find John Mackay on target. After noting that Calvin "became a theologian through his heart," he adds:

> This fact is extremely important for an adequate understanding of Presbyterianism. A system of religious thought and a form of church organization, which were created by a man whose heart was set on fire, cannot be true to their nature unless the reality of a life inflamed with a passion for God and accustomed to communion with God is given a central place. For deep in the heart of Calvinism, and in Presbyterianism in its truest and most classical form, resides a profound piety, that is, a personal experience of God linked to a passionate devotion to God. Piety thus understood provides light and direction for all Christian and humanistic learning. It is piety in this sense that provides the requisite dynamic for the conduct of church affairs and the application of Christianity to life in all its fullness. Piety had been the soul not only of classical Presbyterianism, but also of all genuine Christian witness, whatever be the Confessional family to which a Christian may belong.[31]

SIX

Misunderstanding Six

That the doctrine of predestination is a creation of and unique to the Reformed tradition.

THERE IS NO DENYING that, from the time of Calvin until the present, a hallmark of Reformed theology has been an accent on the sovereignty of God, his gracious election and providence—and predestination.[1] In the never-ending debate about whether the sovereignty of God or the freedom and decision of man should be emphasized, the Calvinist unhesitatingly opts for the former. But no Reformed theologian would ever concede that there is anything fatalistic about this emphasis on the priority of God. A German Reformed scholar, Paul Jacobs, shows that, for Calvin, there is a dialectic but no contradiction between affirming that God is sovereign and that man is still responsible.[2]

Calvin, in any case, is not the inventor of the doctrine of predestination, not even of double predestination, as is often alleged. He has some illustrious predecessors in the apostle Paul, St. Augustine, and Martin Luther.[3] In fact, Luther affirms predestination in terms even stronger than that found in Calvin's writings. According to Luther, predestination is the "dreadful hidden will of God, who, according to His own counsel, ordains such persons as He wills to receive and partake of the mercy preached and offered."[4] Soon after Luther's death (1546), however, his disciples began to soften his views on the subject. By the time of the *Formula of Concord* (1577)—the

Lutheran confession which attempted to settle various controversies—Luther's distinctive views on predestination had been seriously undermined.[5]

Among the various Reformed Churches in the sixteenth century, Calvin's views generally held sway even though there were those in Bern and elsewhere who did not completely agree with them. The last of the great sixteenth-century Reformed confessions, *The Second Helvetic Confession* (1566), was composed by Bullinger, the leader of the Reformed Churches in Zurich. Just two years after Calvin's death, it adopts a view of predestination very similar to Calvin's, but is less explicit about the negative side of predestination (eternal damnation).[6]

> From eternity God has freely, and of his mere grace, without any respect to men, predestinated or elected the saints whom he wills to save in Christ, according to the saying of the apostle, "God chose us in him before the foundation of the world" (Eph. 1:4). And again: "Who saved us and called us with a holy calling, not in virtue of our works but in virtue of his own purpose and the grace which he gave us in Christ Jesus ages ago . . ." (2 Tim. 1:9f.).

Further:

> Therefore, although not on account of any merit of ours, God has elected us, not directly, but in Christ, and on account of Christ, in order that those who are now ingrafted into Christ by faith might also be elected. But those who were outside Christ were rejected. . . .[7]

The doctrine of predestination came to loom large in Calvin's theology because of doctrinal disputes. But, one finds very little on this subject in the first edition of the *Institutes* and only incidental allusions in his *Genevan Catechism*. (The same is true of the *Heidelberg Catechism*. He does treat this doctrine at some length in his first catechism, *The Instruction in Faith*, but here his concern is pastoral and existential, not an abstract discussion of God's decrees.[8] In this catechism, predestination is discussed in the thirteenth chapter: the title of the twelfth chapter is "We Apprehend Christ Through Faith," and the fourteenth chapter deals with "True Faith." The context, here and in the *Institutes,* is significant. Calvin is trying to show why some people believe and others do not. His answer, in short, is that it ultimately depends not on our piety or ability but on God's secret counsel or will. Even in the last edition of the *Institutes* Calvin speaks beautifully of Christ as "the mirror" of our election. If we want to know about our election, we look to him, not to some hidden God. "If we seek God's fatherly mercy and kindly heart," Calvin counsels, "we should turn our eyes to Christ, on whom alone God's Spirit rests" (see Mt 3:17). Calvin then cites Ephesians 1:4—a key text in this connection[9]—and comments, "But if we have been chosen in him, we shall not find assurance of our election in ourselves; and not even in God the Father, if we conceive him as severed from his Son. *Christ, then, is the mirror wherein we must . . . contemplate our own election.*"[10]

It is true that Calvin also taught the doctrine of reprobation, i.e., that God not only chooses certain people to be saved but that he also, by an eternal decree, has condemned others to damnation because of their sins (III.23.1-3). This has never been a very popular doctrine except in very orthodox Calvinist circles. Even Calvin described it as "a dreadful decree" (II.23.7). However, two things must be noted.

First, it is to Calvin's credit that he takes seriously such passages as Romans 9-11. The same cannot be said of some modern commentators, such as C.H. Dodd and A.M. Hunter.[11] This does not mean, however, that Calvin's exegesis is infallible. Even a conservative Dutch Calvinist like G.C. Berkouwer feels that Calvin fails to understand Paul's argument in Romans 9:17f. He feels that Calvin draws unwarranted conclusions regarding the example of the hardening of Pharaoh's heart and his stubbornness. Calvin sees here the revelation of eternal damnation, whereas Berkouwer (and most exegetes) maintains that Paul here "is not concerned primarily to expound on the 'ruin of the wicked' which 'is ordained by his counsel and his will,' but rather to point to God's power and freedom in the history of salvation as He proceeds to manifest His mercy."[12]

Second, Calvin was not as rigid in his teaching on this theme as some of his followers. Charles Williams has put it succinctly and cleverly: "So Augustine's predestination was safe with him, comprehensible in Calvin, tiresome in English Puritans, and quite horrible in Scottish Presbyterians."[13] Likewise, one might add, with some Dutch Calvinists!

We get into serious difficulties and cause needless stumbling blocks whenever we try to explain the mystery of God's sovereignty and human freedom in neat, logical terms. This is one of the problems with scholastic approaches where Aristotelian logic seeks to force biblical paradoxes into a philosophical straitjacket. "Reason *does* have its limitations. It cannot give us answers to certain questions, and the question of predestination is one of these. The fact that God is the sovereign Lord *and* the facts of evil and man's free agency and responsibility are paradoxical realities that can be perceived and held only by faith."[14] Rather, we might better face up to the unresolvable tensions in scripture (as in Phil 2:13) and rest content in God's inscrutable wisdom. Jonathan Edwards may point the way:

> In efficacious grace we are not merely passive, nor yet does God do *some* and we do the *rest*. But God does all, and we do all. God produces all, and we act all. For that is what he produces, viz. our own acts. God is the only proper author and fountain; we only are the proper actors.[15]

To some people this might appear like theological gobbledygook, but there is a profound practical truth at stake here. Skeptics or opponents of the doctrines of God's sovereignty, election, and predestination often reason that to stress God's sovereignty or election cuts the nerve of any will to act. The argument often runs like this: "If God has determined everything beforehand and rules everything by his sovereign will, why should I bother to do anything?" Thus predestination is viewed as a religious form of determinism or fatalism that leaves people mere robots.

Actually, just the opposite is the case. Those people who have no assurance that the universe and our destinies are ordered and governed by a God who is both omnipotent and loving have little or nothing to give them comfort or hope when disaster strikes or things just go badly. However, those Christians who have unswerving confidence in God's sovereign grace (which is the basis of his election and predestination) can forge ahead, even in the midst of great difficulties. They know that they are not alone and that their success and future ultimately depend, not on their strength and determination, but on God. Thus the doctrine of predestination is a stimulus to perseverance, not fatalistic inertia.

This is brought out in a forceful way by James I. Packer:

There is abroad today a widespread suspicion that a robust faith in the absolute sovereignty of God is bound to undermine any adequate sense of human responsibility. . . . In particular, [such a faith] is thought to paralyse evangelism by robbing one both of the motive to evangelize and of the message to evangelize with. . . . I shall try to show that this is nonsense. I shall try to show further that, as far from inhibiting evangelism, faith in the sovereignty of God's government and grace is the only thing that can sustain it, for it is the only thing that can give us the resilience that we need if we are to evangelize boldly and persistently, and not be daunted by temporary setbacks. So far from being weakened by this faith, therefore, evangelism will inevitably be weak and lack staying power without it.[16]

Whatever errors or excesses Calvin and his followers may have committed in this area, the real purpose of the doctrine— at least as far as Calvin was concerned—was to magnify the sovereign, free grace of God.[17] God's grace is dependable. If man determines his own fate, God is reduced to being a bystander in his own creation. A second purpose in stressing this doctrine—not unrelated to the first—is that of comfort and assurance.[18] Since our salvation is grounded in the free grace and mercy of God, we need not be anxious about our status and future as children of God.

> We know that in everything God works for the good of those who love him, who have been called according to his purpose. For those God foreknew he also predestined to be conformed to the likeness of his Son. . . . If God is for us who can be against us? (Rom 8:28-29, 31, NIV).

Chosen in Christ from all eternity (Eph 1:4), what greater security and comfort could there be for the child of God!

SEVEN

Misunderstanding Seven

*That the doctrine of total depravity means that man
is worthless and capable of no good.*

AGAIN, THERE IS SOME BASIS for this misconception. Those who
are in the Reformed tradition generally take a very dim view of
man's capabilities over against God. This is true of all those who
are heirs of Augustine. Augustinians, whether Jansenists* or
Calvinists, take sin very seriously. Who else in our time would
write a 600-page book on sin but a Dutch Calvinist?[1] Ironically,
in the United States, a generally optimistic nation where sin is
not taken so seriously, the subject of sin recently made
headlines, thanks to a book on the subject not by a theologian
but by a psychiatrist![2]

Though they take sin seriously, Calvinists have the reputa-
tion of being aggressive in the economic realm[3] and progressive
in other areas as well. Historically, they have been more
concerned about education, politics, and culture than Anabaptists, Catholics, Lutherans, pietists, or contemporary

---

*Jansenism was a radically Augustinian movement in the Roman Catholic Church in
the seventeenth and eighteenth centuries. The movement is named after a French
bishop, Cornelius Jansen, who opposed the Jesuits and wanted to reform Catholicism
according to the teachings of Augustine. Their teaching was summed up in five points
strikingly similar to the five points of Calvinism formulated at Dort about forty years
earlier, for example, that grace is irresistible and that Christ died only for the elect. The
movement's most famous member was Blaise Pascal (1623-1662), best known for his
Pensees (thoughts).

45

fundamentalists. The Augustinian-Calvinist view, according to H. Richard Niebuhr, is rather that of Christ *transforming* culture.[4] Christ can, must, and will completely convert man and society.

All this notwithstanding, one of the five points of Calvinism is usually described as "total depravity." This has fostered the view that Calvinists see nothing good in man. This terminology comes neither from Calvin[5] nor from the later *Canons of Dort* (1619), but became popular in later seventeenth- and eighteenth-century disputes with Arminians.[6] Not even the *Westminster Confession* of 1646 uses this terminology, although an equally radical view of sin is held. Here we read instead that due to the sin of "our first parents" they "became dead in sin, and *wholly defiled* in all the faculties and parts of the soul and body" (VI,2). Further, "from this original corruption, whereby we are *utterly indisposed*, disabled, and made opposite to all good, and *wholly inclined* to all evil, do proceed all actual transgressions" (VI, 4). Elsewhere, in the chapter on free will, we have similar language: "Man, by his fall into a state of sin, hath *wholly lost* all ability of will to any spiritual good accompanying salvation" (IX,3, emphasis mine throughout). Whereas the words "total depravity" are nowhere found in the *Westminster Confession*, we do have similar language. It might be more apt, if not more biblical, to speak of the *total inability* of man rather than of his total depravity.

The conviction that man is not free to choose God and that his will is bound is common to Augustine, Luther, and many others in addition to Calvin and the Reformed standards. However, this view is emphasized so strongly and consistently in the Reformed tradition that it has come to be regarded by many as peculiar to us. This is understandable. The title, for example, of a key chapter dealing with man in Calvin's *Institutes* reads: "Only damnable things come forth from man's corrupt nature" (II.3). The *Canons of Dort* describe our condition in equally strong language: "As a result [of the fall], all men are conceived in sin and born as children of wrath, incapable of any saving good, prone to evil, dead in sin and slaves of sin."[7] Even the irenic *Heidelberg Catechism* maintains that "by nature I am prone to hate God and my neighbor" (Question 5). This is a bit strong, but it must be conceded that scripture itself appears to be unequivocal on this matter. "They have all gone astray, they are all alike corrupt; there is none that does good, no not one" (Ps 124:3). "The heart is deceitful above all things, and desperately corrupt" (Jer 17:9. Cf. New Testament passages like Jn 8:34 and Rom 8:7).

Not surprisingly, many Calvinists have concluded that man is indeed worthless and capable of nothing good. Unfortunately, very few people are aware of a crucial distinction which Calvin himself makes concerning fallen man. In the *Institutes,* he distinguishes between man's knowledge and achievements in the realm of "heavenly things" in contrast to the realm of "earthly things" (II.2.13). In the former realm, there is indeed nothing positive of good which the natural man can do. As far as spiritual things are concerned, even "the greatest geniuses are blinder than moles" (II.2.18). Apart from the grace of God and the help of his spirit, "we are utterly blind and stupid in divine matters" (II.2.19). In this, the vertical dimension, there is no question that man's depravity is indeed "total."

Interestingly, the preponderant source of Calvin's scriptural citations in these sections of the *Institutes* is the New Testament, not the Old. In particular, he appeals to John's Gospel and 1 Corinthians.

The light shines in the darkness and the darkness has not understood it. (Jn 1:5, NIV)

No one can receive anything except what is given him from heaven. (Jn 3:27)

No one can come to me unless the Father who sent me draws him. (Jn 6:44)

The unspiritual man does not receive the gifts of the Spirit of God, for they are folly to him, and he is not able to understand them because they are spiritually discerned.
(1 Cor 2:14; cf. 1 Cor 1:20 and 2:9)

However, Calvin takes a much more positive view of man's capabilities and gifts on the horizontal level.[8] In what we would call the secular realm (i.e., of "earthly things"), even fallen man possesses a degree of conscience, common sense, natural instinct, reason, sense of justice and equity, as well as general ability in the realms of government, household management, mechanical skills, and the liberal arts (II.2.13, cf. II.14-17). These natural gifts are corrupted through sin (II.2.12), but they are not to be denigrated. Thanks to God's "general grace" (II.2.17),[9] "some sparks still gleam" in "man's perverted and degenerate nature."[10] There is also in sinful man "some sort of desire to search out the truth . . ." (II.2.12).[11]

The results of this universal kindness of God toward all men are not insignificant. Calvin had a high regard for the accomplishments and insights of "pagans" like Plato and Cicero, of whom he wrote: "Let that admirable light of truth shining in them teach us that the mind of man, though fallen and perverted from its wholeness, is nevertheless clothed and ornamented with God's excellent gifts" (II.2.15). Too often a false Puritan-pietistic reaction of certain Christians has been to reject the "worldly" accomplishments of a Beethoven, an Einstein, or a Van Gogh. To this attitude Calvin replies: "If we regard the Spirit of God as the sole fountain of truth itself, we shall neither reject the truth itself, nor despise it wherever it shall appear, unless we wish to dishonor the Spirit of God. For by holding the gifts of the Spirit in slight esteem, we condemn and reproach the Spirit himself" (ibid.). In the words of Paul, "Whatever is true, whatever is honorable, whatever is just, whatever is pure, whatever is lovely, whatever is gracious, if there is any excellence, if there is anything worthy of praise, think about these things" (Phil 4:8).

Thus Will Durant, the popular American historian, is completely wrong in asserting that Calvin "completely rejected the humanist concern with earthly excellence . . ."[12] Much more accurate is the judgment of H. Richard Niebuhr, who refers to Calvin's "more humanistic [than Luther's] views of the splendor of human nature still evident in the ruins of the fall."[13]

Hence, we must be careful when we use the expression "total depravity." It is a true description insofar as it suggests that there is no part of our nature that is not affected by sin: our reason, our wills, and our bodies. Moreover, there is nothing we can do to make ourselves right with God. All is of grace. Nevertheless, as a Christian Reformed commentator points out, "The word 'total' must not be taken in an absolute sense as though man is completely depraved. Man is not as bad as he can be."[14] More recently, another Christian Reformed scholar, Cornelius Plantinga, recognizing that the *Canons of Dort* do not use the term *total depravity* comments:

> The phrase "total depravity" . . . has often led people to think Calvinists were radical pessimists or even misanthropes. That is a mistake. The Canons nowhere say that unregenerate people always do what is utterly wrong. There is no suggestion that if an atheist has a choice between hugging his children and throttling them he will throttle them every time. Nothing of the sort. . . . Unregenerate people often know the difference between good and evil and show "some regard for virtue."[15]

From a Reformed standpoint, therefore, there is a legitimate place for appreciation of so-called secular or non-Christian achievements. Man, for all his perversity, is not a wretched worm capable only of evil.[16] By the grace of God he can do some things worthy of admiration and praise.

Moreover, to think of a Christian in such terms is an insult to the transforming power of the gospel. If Christians are "a new creation" (2 Cor 5:17), it is totally inappropriate to think of such persons in terms of their past. This does not mean that the battle with sin and the powers of evil is over. Our new life in Christ is always "covered by a deep shadow,"[17] but the important thing to be remembered here is that sin is "no longer the sphere of power in which believers must live."[18] "It is," therefore, "not correct to describe a regenerate person as someone who is still 'depraved' or even 'totally depraved.' Though such a person did share in this depravity by nature, 'something new' has been added . . . the indwelling Christ.''[19]

Note, however, that this is due to the grace of God. There is no place for pride and arrogance on the part of man. Our proper attitude should be one of gratitude to God, who in his infinite mercy has allowed even his rebellious creatures to retain a remnant of the gifts originally bestowed on them (I.15.1 and II.2.14-17).[20] The one who is "in Christ" and has received his Spirit is even more indebted to God and his infinite mercy and grace. Calvin's purpose, in urging us to give due recognition to natural man's achievements and growth in grace on the part of the regenerate person is to glorify God, not man.

EIGHT

Misunderstanding Eight

*That the Reformed faith fosters a negative, legalistic
approach to the Christian life.*

THIS MISUNDERSTANDING originates in a long-standing popular
caricature of Calvin. Because of the strict disciplinary measures
which were enforced in Geneva, it is frequently assumed—even
by noted historians and theologians—that Calvin's theology
must be legalistic and lacking in any real appreciation of
Christian freedom and the joy of the gospel. This, combined
with the image of Calvin as *the* theologian of double predestination and the one who burned Servetus* (technically incorrect;
Calvin was opposed to this form of execution),[1] creates a picture
of Calvin as a dour, grim figure who interpreted the Bible
literalistically as a law-book. He is accordingly dismissed as a
"law-teacher" (*Gesetzlehrer*) who knew little of the love and
grace of God.[2]

---

*Michael Servetus was a marked man in both Catholic and Protestant circles for his
heretical views. He came to Geneva in 1553, partly to challenge Calvin's authority
which at this time was at a low point. Servetus was discovered, imprisoned, and, after a
trial, condemned to death by burning. Calvin favored his execution—as did all of the
other major Protestant church leaders in Europe—but pleaded with the city council to
have Servetus killed by a less cruel method. The council would not relent. Calvin's
detractors point to this as a terrible blemish on his record, but fail to recognize that the
execution of heretics was common in those times and for at least two centuries
afterward. Zurich Protestants drowned Anabaptists, Lutherans killed Reformed,
Anglicans executed dissidents, and there was the Catholic Inquisition. This does not
justify such acts, but it does place them in historical perspective.

Since World War II, Reformation and Calvin studies have done much to undercut these myths concerning Calvin, but popular caricatures die hard.[3] There has been a growing appreciation of Calvin's understanding of the law in many recent works on Christian ethics. However, an English scholar can still repeat the charge that in "Calvin's thought in particular and in Reformed teaching in general" there is a "fundamentalist strain"[4] (i.e., a literalistic approach to scripture when dealing with ethical problems).

Unfortunately, Reformed/Presbyterian Churches have usually done little to allay this suspicion. This is especially so in the Netherlands, Scotland, and the United States. But even in Germany it is reputed that one can distinguish between Reformed and Lutheran Christians by the fact that the former "endure" whereas the latter "enjoy" their religion. Bonhoeffer might justly charge his Lutheran compatriots with an unbiblical notion of "cheap grace," but on the Reformed side one could level the charge of "no grace"—merely good works.

In many Dutch-American Reformed Churches and Scottish-American Presbyterian Churches, sabbatarianism and other forms of legalism have certainly been all too characteristic of faith and piety. A good Christian was one who went to church twice on Sunday, did not do anything else on "the Sabbath" except take naps and read Christian literature, and one who during the week stayed away from worldly amusements such as the tavern, theater, and dance hall. (Here there is an overlapping with the fundamentalists, although many Dutch-Americans drank, smoked, and did not have very good records regarding premarital sex.) A further characteristic was great emphasis on purity of doctrine with little corresponding emphasis on the fruit of the Spirit and the joy of the Lord.

There has been considerable improvement in many of these areas in recent years. In order to make further progress, we must purge some of the unhappy influence of Pietism and Puritanism which invaded the Reformed bloodstream. A rediscovery of Calvin's understanding of the law, Christian freedom, and the Christian life will help us to recover a more biblical approach.

The legalistic tendency in the Reformed tradition has no basis or antecedent in Calvin's theology of the law.[5] He did, indeed, stress the so-called "third use of the law" as being the "principal" and "proper" use or function of the law* (II.7.12). Here the law no longer condemns and accuses but comes to the believer as a law fulfilled in Christ. It is now a norm and guide for the Christian life.[6] A stress on the continuing, normative function of the law can lead to an overconcern with law and to legalism. While possible, it is not likely in Calvin's approach to law. His principles of interpretation of the law—especially the Ten Commandments—if taken seriously, should prevent any unevangelical literalism or legalism.

First, Calvin notes that the law is spiritual (see Rom 7:14); therefore, its commands must be spiritually understood and interpreted. For "God is concerned not so much with outward appearance as with purity of heart" (II.8.6). In emphasizing "inward and spiritual righteousness" in contrast to external observance Calvin insists that he is only "following Christ, its [the law's] best interpreter" (II.8.7).

Second, since most of the commandments are negative and necessarily limited in their expression of God's will, we must attempt to discover God's real intention in each commandment and interpret it positively in the light of God's will revealed in scripture.[7] "The commandments and prohibitions always contain more than is expressed in words," Calvin observes, and hence anyone who "confines his understanding of the law

---

*On the three uses of the law see the II.7.6-15. The first function of the law, according to Calvin, is to make us aware of our sinfulness so that we will flee to God's grace. The second function is the external use of the law by the state to keep order and justice. The third use of the law is as teacher, or trainer. Luther reversed the order of the first two uses, but taught essentially the same thing. He did not explicitly teach a third use, but his treatment of the decalogue in his *Larger Catechism* is much the same as Calvin's. Moreover, the third use is taught in the Lutheran *Formula of Concord* and continues to be maintained by many Lutheran pietists. Even so, from the latter part of the sixteenth century and down to the present this has been one of the major points of tension between Lutheran and Reformed Churches.

within the narrowness of the words deserves to be laughed at" (II.8.8). This rule of interpretation alone undercuts all the charges of Calvin's approach to the law being literalistic or fundamentalistic!

Third, the Ten Commandments should be considered from the perspective of the two great commandments which direct us to the love of God and neighbor. The law thereby comprehends the whole of life in both its vertical and horizontal dimensions. If anyone imagines that Calvin says little about Christian love, he should examine Calvin's full and enthusiastic discussions of the sum of the law following his expositions of the various commandments in his catechisms, his commentary, and the *Institutes.* Calvin's concern about the law is ultimately a concern for the love of God and our fellow man. Hence he frequently refers to the law as a "rule of love" (II.8.49).

Calvin's approach to the law is, thus, thoroughly evangelical in that he sees it through the eyes of Christ. His understanding of the law does not, as has been alleged, reflect an "Old Testament religion," but rather breathes the spirit of the Sermon on the Mount.[8] Equally important is his insistence that Jesus Christ is the heart, soul, life, spirit, purpose, and fulfillment of the law.[9] "Indeed, every doctrine of the law, every command, every promise, always points to Christ. We are, therefore, to apply all its parts to him. . . . No one will be able to understand the law correctly who does not constantly strive to attain this mark."[10]

Mention should be made of Calvin's interpretation of the Sabbath commandment, since it is here above all that Reformed Churches have been guilty of so much nonsense. Calvin's discussion of the commandment is completely free of any legalistic sabbatarianism. In fact, in a recent study of the Lord's Day by Professor Jewett of Fuller Seminary, the complaint is that Calvin is too vague and pragmatic in his interpretation of this commandment![11] The heart of the Lord's Day, for Calvin, consists not in certain requirements and prohibitions but in a profound symbolical and spiritual experience which points to God's eternal rest. Its primary purpose is that we cease from our works in order that God may work in us by his Spirit (II.8.28,29,34).

In light of all this it is difficult to know exactly where Calvinists began to go astray in this matter of law and the Christian life.[12]

Another insight of Calvin's that was also soon forgotten was that the law must not be isolated from its original context, viz., the covenant of grace. Calvin sees great significance in the preface to the Decalogue: "I am the Lord, your God, who brought you out of the land of Egypt, out of the house of bondage." The Ten Commandments *follow*, not precede, this redemptive act of God. The law, originally, was not a means by which the Israelites were to achieve their salvation, but rather a gift to a people already redeemed.[13] Law and grace are not antithetical, but just the opposite. The law is first of all a gift of grace, not a demand. Abstract the law, however, from its proper context of the covenant of grace, and it withers into bare, moralistic precepts. This has happened too often in the Reformed tradition.

Calvin often warns against the sin of ingratitude, which occurs when we fail to respond to God's goodness and grace with an appropriate love and obedience of faith. In this connection, we should recall the structure of the *Heidelberg Catechism.* Part I deals with man's sin and guilt. However, the law in this section consists of the two great love commandments, not the Decalogue, lest anyone imagine that he could fulfill the law. The Ten Commandments are not discussed until Part III, which deals with man's gratitude and obedience. With Calvin, the proper motivation for ethical behavior is not a sense of obligation and compulsion but of gratitude. The only obedience which counts in God's eyes is that which stems from a loving, grateful heart.[14]

We should not leave this subject without mentioning Christian freedom. This was one of the great gifts of the gospel which the apostle Paul prized and valiantly defended (see Rom 6:15f; Gal 5:1-13; cf. Jn 8:32; 1 Pt 2:16). It was also a major theme of the reformers. One of Luther's most famous and influential tracts was "The Freedom of the Christian Man." However, Christian freedom has hardly been a hallmark of the later Reformed tradition, which has tended to be authoritarian.

Again, this is not Calvin's fault. His chapter on Christian freedom in the *Institutes* (III.19) has been rightly described as "a jewel" by Paul Wernle, a prominent Swiss scholar of a past generation. Wernle goes on to say: "How many words about Calvin's legalism would have remained unspoken if this chapter had been read more often."[15]

Calvin's opening lines are worth repeating: "He who proposes to summarize the gospel teaching ought by no means to omit an explanation of this topic . . . for unless freedom is comprehended, neither Christ nor gospel truth, nor inner peace of soul can be rightly known" (III.19.1). Calvin proceeds to discuss at considerable length freedom from the law and freedom of conscience. Freedom from the law, however, is freedom from the power and curse of the law, not freedom from the righteousness which God still desires in his children. Even here, however, there is a difference between the righteousness of the law and that which is received through faith in Christ. A troubled conscience, in any case, should look not to the law but to "God's mercy alone" and "only to Christ" (III.19.2).

This is only one aspect of Christian freedom. For the rest, one should read this chapter himself—and several times—in order to appreciate the riches it contains. Only one further point in conclusion: The purpose of our freedom, Calvin observes, is ultimately positive.

We are not simply freed from the curse of the law and from a bad conscience. We are free now to love and to serve without fear and without compulsion. We are free to "use God's gifts for the purpose for which he gave them to us, with no scruple of conscience and no trouble of mind. With such confidence our minds will be at peace with him, and will recognize his liberality toward us" (III.19.8).[16]

This approach and this spirit are a part of our Reformed heritage. It is about time we discovered and appropriated it.

NINE

Misunderstanding Nine

*That the covenant concept produces a sense
of pride and exclusiveness.*

REFORMED THEOLOGY is covenant theology. In the words of the
Westminster Larger Catechism, the God of scripture is "a God in
Covenant" (Q. 101). This is a true statement as long as the term
"covenant theology" is not limited to the special form of
covenant theology (also known as federal theology) which
developed in the seventeenth century. The idea of a covenant, of
course, is a thoroughly biblical notion. In fact, one of the
greatest Old Testament scholars of our time, Walther Eichrodt,
maintains that the covenant concept is the central theme of the
Old Testament.[1]

Even so, it is in Reformed theology that the covenant idea was
emphasized and developed. Prior to Calvin, the Zurich reformer, Zwingli, had begun to develop a theology of the
covenant, and his successor, H. Bullinger, along with Calvin,
developed the notion even further.[2] Ursinus, one of the authors
of the *Heidelberg Catechism,* also promoted a covenantal concept
of God's redemptive revelation. Thus, even before the forma-
tion of a special "covenant theology" by Coccejus (1603-1669)
in the seventeenth century, emphasis on the covenant had
become one of the distinguishing features of Reformed theology.[3]

The effects of covenant theology in Europe and America in
the seventeenth and eighteenth centuries are not our present

concern, but there have been at least two unhappy develop-
ments in more recent times in Dutch Calvinist circles. (In the
Presbyterian Churches the chief influence has been the impact
of the notion of a covenant of works on the Westminister
theology as found in the *Westminster Confession* and the
Westminster Larger Catechism. Many Presbyterian scholars
regard this as an unfortunate development.[4]) In the Netherlands and United States, stress on the covenant concept has
unfortunately often resulted in an exclusivistic mentality which
regarded all covenant (i.e., Reformed) people as especially
within the sphere of God's grace and all non-Calvinists as, in a
sense, outside the fold. This attitude was accentuated by
Abraham Kuyper's idea of sphere sovereignty which resulted in
Christian (i.e., Calvinist) political parties, trade unions, and
even Christian goat-breeding societies![5] His heirs in the
Netherlands and in the United States—in the Christian
Reformed Church in particular—have accordingly developed
Christian schools as well. It is in this context that one often
heard in the past much talk about "our covenant children," etc.
Inevitably, a "we-they" type of mentality developed in certain
areas.

That this is still something of a problem in Christian school
circles is apparent in a column, "Principal's Perspective," by
George Groen in the magazine *The Christian Educator's
Journal.* In one issue, he shares the results of a questionnaire
sent to school administrators in a given district in the fall of
1976.[6] Here are some of the concerns which surfaced:

> Many "foreign phrases" in our enrollment information
> may have little or no meaning to the non-Reformed Chris-
> tian.
>
> If parents from Reformed and Christian Reformed
> churches were screened as closely as parents from non-
> supporting churches, we would have to release several
> families now in our schools.
>
> Teachers tend to have "tunnel vision" when they accept

children of other faiths [i.e., non-covenantal children!]

I wonder [a school principal's response] if we really know how the non-Reformed parent feels when he tries to have his child admitted?

These comments indicate that many Christian school administrators and teachers are aware of and sensitive to the problems that arise when we distinguish too self-consciously between our covenant children and those (Gentile?) children who do not quite belong, even when they are from Christian homes.

The term *Dutch Calvinists* has become a term of special opprobrium on an international level because of quite another phenomenon, indirectly derived from a false application of the covenant concept. In South Africa, the Dutch Reformed Churches have tried to give a theological justification for their national policy of *apartheid*. Since they are Calvinists, it is sometimes assumed that their rationale for separateness derives from Reformed theology in general, and the covenant concept in particular.[7] Trevor Huddleston, for example, in his widely read book, *Naught for Your Comfort*, blames Calvinism for providing the ideological basis for South Africa's racial policies.

Is there perhaps some truth in the idea that an emphasis upon the covenant produces a superior, separatist mentality? Historically, there might seem to be some basis for this conclusion. To the extent that this is so, I suspect it derives from a certain type of federal theology, not from the covenant idea as developed by the early sixteenth-century reformers. For in federal theology[8] used in the technical sense, it is taught that in the Bible there are *two* major covenants which God made with man: a covenant of works made with Adam and a covenant of grace in Jesus Christ. According to this approach, since Adam failed to keep the agreement which God made with him at creation, it was necessary for God to enter into a second agreement with Christ on behalf of the elect.

Amazingly, this unbiblical notion became the organizing principle of later Reformed and Puritan theologies. There were terminological variations such as Gomarus's* distinction between a "natural" and a "supernatural covenant," but the fatal division remained. The basic biblical notion of one covenant, and that a covenant of grace, was obscured for centuries. Happily, the idea of a covenant of works is not taught in the later *Canons of Dort*. It is found explicitly, however, in the *Westminster Confession* (VII, 2,3), another seventeenth-century product.[9] It was later promoted in the Netherlands by Kuyper and Bavinck and in the United States through the influential theologies of Charles and A.A. Hodge. It continues to make inroads in American Reformed circles through Berkhof's *Systematic Theology*.[10]

One of the first in Reformed Church circles to protest against this unbiblical notion was Albertus Pieters. Much of his career and his retirement was spent fighting this notion and the legalism related to it. He also sounded the alarm against the pernicious consequences of a dispensational approach to scripture taught in the Scofield Bible and in many American Bible institutes and seminaries.[11]

More recently, the late John Murray, the Scottish theologian who taught for many years at Westminster Seminary in Philadelphia, has demonstrated in a helpful monograph that the Bible teaches basically only one covenant, a covenant of grace.[12] The covenant takes on many forms, for God covenanted with Noah (Gn 9:9-17), Abraham (Gn 15:8-18, 17:1-14), Moses (Ex 6:2-8, 19:3-6, 24:1-8), and David (2 Sm 7:12-17; cf. Ps 89:3-4). There is also promise of "a new covenant" (Jer 21:21-24; Ez 11:17-20) which is fulfilled in Jesus Christ (Heb 8:8-12, 10:16-17). However, the essence or substance of the covenant remains the same; it is only the administration that varies (II.10.2). The promise is always the same: "I will be your God and you shall be my people" (Ex 6:7; Lv 26:12; Jer 31:33; 2 Cor 6:16; Heb 8:10; Rv 21:3).

Thus, "from the beginning of God's disclosures to men in

---

*Gomarus (or Gomar) was the leading Calvinist theologian in the dispute with the Arminians in the early seventeenth century and played a prominent role at the Synod of Dort (1618-1619).

terms of covenant we find a unity of conception which is to the effect that a divine covenant is a sovereign administration of grace and promise. It is not compact or contract or agreement that provides the constitutive or governing idea but that of dispensation in the sense of disposition."[13] There are always stipulations; faith, love, and obedience are always corollaries. But the covenant promise remains. Moreover, we eventually read of an "everlasting covenant" because it has been ratified in the blood of Christ (Jer 32:40; 1 Cor 11:25; Heb 13:20).

The important thing to keep in mind is that God's covenant companionship with his people rests on his gracious election. By his unfathomable grace he takes us to himself in a veritable partner-like relationship. "It expresses the union of God and man."[14] God initiates the relationship, invites man into an enduring fellowship with him, and commits himself in love and grace to an unworthy people, who are then to respond in gratitude and love.

There is, of course, particularity here. God does not so covenant with everyone. God's covenant people are "a chosen race, a royal priesthood, a holy nation, God's own people" (1 Pt 2:9a). Hence, the constant danger of a proud, exclusivistic spirit.[15] Those who enjoy this unique covenant relationship with God must always remind themselves that it is the Lord of history who determines the scope and bounds of the covenant. It is not a private club or an elite group, worthy or superior in any way (see 1 Cor 1:26-30; Rom 9:25-26). In the Old Testament, the covenant association "draws no clear line to exclude the stranger, but is continually absorbing outsiders to itself."[16]

Rightly interpreted, the covenant concept is not only a profound biblical motif with far-reaching hermeneutical and theological implications, but also a concept which has revolutionary possibilities. Some of these were discussed recently by representatives of the World Alliance of Reformed Churches who explored the theme, "A Covenant Challenge to Our Broken World." Here churchmen, biblical scholars, and theologians such as Jorge Lara-Braud, Walter Brueggeman, Arthur

TEN

Misunderstanding Ten

That to be Reformed means to be indifferent
or opposed to the so-called "worldly" realms of
culture, economics, and politics, and to be concerned
only about the salvation of souls.

IN AN EARLIER VERSION of this book, this chapter had a simpler—
and somewhat misleading—title, namely, "That to be Reformed means to be opposed to the world and be concerned only
about one's own salvation." This was misleading because of the
different meanings of the key word *world*. I was using the word
in its more comprehensive, neutral meaning. *World* in this sense
meant not only "the realms of culture, economics, and politics,"
but also comprehended the whole created order and life
within it.

The Bible often speaks of the "world" in this way. "God so
loved the *world* that he gave his only Son . . ." (Jn 3:16a; cf. 1 Jn
4:9). Christ is the "Savior of the world" (Jn 4:43, 12:47; 1 Jn
4:14). The world has also been reconciled to God through
Christ (2 Cor 5:19). Thus "the kingdom of the world has
become the kingdom of our Lord and of his Christ" (Rv 11:15).
This is why we sing, "This is my Father's world." God not only
created the world but loves it and cares for it despite its sin and
rebellion. In this sense, we too are to care for the world, be
concerned about it, and become involved in it for its better-
ment—for God's sake! "For everything created by God is good,

63

and nothing is to be rejected if it is received with thanksgiving" (1 Tm 4:4).

However, in the majority of New Testament references to the "world" the meaning is negative. Particularly in the Johannine and Pauline writings the "world" is primarily the sphere which is at enmity with God. "The whole world is in the power of the evil one" (1 Jn 5:19). The devil is regarded as "the ruler of this world" (Jn 12:31, 14:30, 16:11). The world hated Jesus and will similarly hate his followers (Jn 7:7, 15:18-19, 17:14; 1 Jn 3:13). Understood in this way, through the cross of Christ "the world has been crucified" to us and we in turn "to the world" (Gal 6:14). Accordingly, James says "religion that is pure and undefiled before God" is "to keep oneself unstained from the world" (Jas 4:4).

Because of this strong motif in the New Testament many Christians have concluded that they should withdraw from the world or oppose it strenuously as the realm of the devil. They have not, however, paid sufficient attention to Jesus' high priestly prayer—also in John's Gospel—that his heavenly Father not take his disciples "out of the world." True, they are "not of the world," but Jesus sends them "into the world" (Jn 17:15-17). While, on the one hand, Christians are to remain "unstained from the world," they are at the same time "the salt of the earth" and "the light of the world" (Mt 5:13, 14).

Historically, Reformed Christians have taken this mandate of their Lord's seriously. Therefore, they have seen the world not only as the realm of the evil one but also as that sphere in which God is seeking to bring about a kingdom that comprehends more than individual Christians, or even the church. This is why Reformed Christians often speak of a (*Weltanschauung*).*

Yet, in recent times in particular, one hears from many Reformed/Presbyterian Christians that we should get out of

---

*The expression *Weltanschauung* is German, but the phrase "life and world view" is very popular among the Dutch-American Calvinists, particularly those who have been influenced by Abraham Kuyper. It is significant that he begins his *Lectures on Calvinism* with a lecture on "Calvinism, a Life System." "Life-system" is simply a shortened form of the free translation of *Weltanschauung* as "life and world view."

politics, avoid controversial social issues, and stick to the proper business of the church, namely, preaching the gospel for the purpose of saving souls. Without realizing it, such Christians reflect more of a pietistic-fundamentalist outlook and spirit than that of the Reformed tradition. (The same could not be said of the early evangelical movement, which combined evangelistic fervor with a keen social conscience—unlike most contemporary conservative evangelicals.[1]) Such people are suspicious of—or even vehemently hostile to—efforts of the church to speak to or become involved in social, economic, or political affairs. If their ministers speak from the pulpit to challenge local practices or convictions on subjects such as race, fair housing, nuclear arms—they are told to stick to the gospel and not meddle in secular affairs. Similarly, when denominational agencies or organizations like the National Council of Churches make pronouncements on such issues, many Reformed Christians protest that the business of the church is evangelism, not social or political matters.

This attitude is not limited to those of Reformed/ Presbyterian backgrounds. It is characteristic of most conservative, evangelical American Protestants. There has been a curious twist in the 1980s with the rise of the Christian New Right and groups like the Moral Majority, headed by Jerry Falwell.[2] In the past, the so-called social gospel and political activism were viewed as the domain of theological liberals. Now we have the fascinating phenomenon of fundamentalists and conservatives of various denominational backgrounds (including Jews and Roman Catholics[3]) uniting to form an influential block which claims credit for the defeat of Jimmy Carter and various liberal congressmen in the 1980 national elections.

The tactics—and often the goals—of the Moral Majority and similar groups representative of the New Right have been denounced by leaders of many of the mainline denominations, including the House of Bishops of the Episcopal Church.[4] The charge is that religious representatives of the New Right oversimplify the issues, confuse piety and patriotism, and threaten religious freedom. Also, the "morality" of the Moral

Majority is confined to issues like abortion, gay rights, pornography, and prayer in the schools. The "morality" of their critics (including Catholic bishops) includes civil rights, peace, poverty, and hunger as well as the former issues. On some issues, there is common concern: the arms race and national defense, for example. But, there the viewpoints are diametrically opposed!

In the Reformed tradition, in any case, there has usually been an avoidance of either extremes—social activism devoid of solid theological underpinnings or uncritical identification with right-wing causes. Yet, it must be conceded that in more recent times there has been a tendency, by Reformed/Presbyterian lay people in particular, to protest against ecclesiastical expressions of concern about social, economic, and political issues, except for those that have to do with personal morality. When Reformed Christians espouse such narrow and negative views about the church's mission and relationship to the world they are betraying the best of their heritage. Furthermore, those who think this way only reveal how much the Reformed tradition has been infiltrated by alien elements.

To be Reformed does not require that one agree with or countenance all that transpires in the political-economic realm in the name of the church or a Christian organization. Sometimes pronouncements issued by social-action groups representing denominations or church councils reflect prevailing liberal attitudes more than the mind of Christ.[5] Too often—especially in the activistic, radical 1960s—social action and involvement were hailed as the only authentic form of Christian witness, whereas personal evangelism, foreign missions, traditional worship, preaching, and Bible study were all dismissed as irrelevant and passé.

Historic Reformed Christianity acknowledges no such bifurcation. It recognizes no either/or between evangelism and social action, worship and service. At its best, the Reformed tradition has promoted and held together a warm personal piety and high churchmanship with a full-orbed concern for the world in its social and cultural as well as its economic and political dimensions. Precisely because it has taken seriously the Word of God in its entirety, it has not ignored the concern for social righteousness so prominent in the prophets (and by no means neglected by our Lord). Nor has it pitted the message of James (good works) against that of Galatians (justification by faith). To be Reformed is to seek to bring the whole gospel to the whole world, not a truncated version which applies only to the individual's spiritual welfare. Reformed theology is kingdom theology.[6] Its concerns, like those of the scriptures, go beyond the church as well as the individual. This biblical motif is frequently neglected or overlooked in evangelical circles despite the fact that the central theme of Jesus' preaching in the synoptic gospels is the coming of the kingdom of God.[7] When Jesus began his public ministry in Galilee, his message, in a nutshell, was: "The time is fulfilled, and the kingdom of God is at hand; repent and believe the gospel" (Mk 1:15; cf. Mt 12:17; Lk 4:43). We also read of Paul that, toward the end of his career in Rome, in response to Jewish inquirers, he tried to convince them that Jesus was the Messiah, "testifying to the kingdom of God" (Acts 28:23).

The kingdom of God, both a present and coming reality, points to the rule of Christ over the principalities and powers as well as over the believer and the church. This great vision of the Bible has long been of special interest in the Reformed theological world—more than in Anglican or Lutheran theology or in Wesleyan-Baptist individualist types of piety. Representative of this interest is the recent theological treatment of the kingdom by the RCA pastor-theologian, Isaac Rottenberg: *The Promise and the Presence: Toward a Theology of the Kingdom of God.*[8] A disciple of the late A.A. van Ruler and one of the most influential Dutch theologians in the Netherlands in our time, Rottenberg stresses, on the one hand, that the kingdom concept keeps pointing us to the future, but, on the other hand, that "God the Creator is recreating the world."[9] The church in such a theology is not identified with the kingdom but is rather viewed as "a sign of the kingdom."[10] Then, not only the church but also the world becomes a concern for the Christian.

From John Calvin to the late A.A. van Ruler,[11] there has been a beautiful blending of a robust individual piety with a very practical concern for an involvement in the world. Calvin begins his *Institutes* with a discussion of how we can know God. He stresses the necessity of having a genuine piety, i.e., faith, love, reverence, and the fear of God (I.2.1,2). He ends the *Institutes,* however, not in the manner of a traditional dogmatic treatise with a discussion of last things (heaven and hell, the resurrection, etc.) but with a powerful chapter on the civil magistrate! Calvin saw the state as a divinely appointed agency which, along with the church, was a means toward establishing God's order in the world. In Geneva, he not only preached several days each week and continually lectured on the Bible, but he also showed concern for such mundane matters as interest rates, sewers, safety features in homes, and immigration policies. He also established an academy which was to become the University of Geneva. His goal was to manifest the lordship of Christ in every sphere of life.[12]

A more modern example is Abraham Kuyper (1837-1920), not only one of the greatest Dutch theologians of all time but also prime minister in the Netherlands for a brief period and an organizer of the Free University in Amsterdam. *Lectures on Calvinism* reveal something of the scope of his Christian vision. Instead of expounding the five points of Calvinism (total depravity, unconditional election, limited atonement, irresistible grace, and the perseverance of the saints)[13] he dealt with such subjects as "Calvinism and Politics," "Calvinism and Science," "Calvinism and Art." Here, too, is a genuine recognition of God as sovereign not only over the soul but over every sphere of life.

An illustration of this—in addition to the social and political concerns already noted—is the interest in the arts in the Reformed tradition. A contemporary classic in this field is Gerardus van der Leeuw's *Sacred and Profane Beauty: The Holy in Art.*[14] This is, in effect, a theological aesthetics which examines all the arts—drama, dance, literature, painting, sculpture, architecture,[15] music—from a religious perspective. Van der Leeuw, the late Professor of the History of Religion at the University of Groningen (the Netherlands), was considered the most important scientific historian of religion in his generation.

On the American scene, Reformed and Presbyterian scholars have also made significant contributions in this field.[16] Two of these scholars find their inspiration in the Kuyperian tradition and belong to the Christian Reformed Church. Both of their books appeared in 1980, and both deal with art in the larger framework of a Christian aesthetic. The one, *Rainbows for the Fallen World: Aesthetic Life and Artistic Task*,[17] is by Calvin Seerveld, senior member in philosophical aesthetics at the Institute for Christian Studies in Toronto. The other, *Art in Action: Toward a Christian Aesthetic*,[18] is by Nicholas Wolterstorff, professor of philosophy at Calvin College.

Both of these scholars are, in effect carrying out the "cultural mandate," a popular idea in neo-Calvinist (i.e., Kuyperian) circles. This idea is derived from the creation mandate in Genesis 1:28: "God said to [Adam and Eve] 'Be fruitful and multiply, and fill the earth and subdue it; and have dominion over . . . every living thing.'" In this command is the justification for the development of culture, which is therefore "not a peripheral concern, but of the very essence of life."[19] This is why, according to Seerveld, "*aesthetic obedience* is required of everyone by the Lord," whereas only a few are given artistic talent.[20]

In 1980, another significant study of art from a Christian perspective appeared, *Signs of Our Times: Theological Essays on Art in the Twentieth Century*[21] by George S. Heyer, associate professor of theology at Austin Presbyterian Theological Seminary in Texas. Heyer's background is quite different from that of Seerveld and Wolterstorff, but he too is captivated by "art's true potency—the expression of a God-given gift whose exercise can immeasurably enrich human life." In contrast to Dutch-style neo-Calvinists, Heyer does not see the "cultural mandate" in terms of a creation mandate. Art and culture express both the power and beauty that come from the Spirit of the Father and the Son.[22] In these studies we see impressive examples of the Calvinist concern for culture.

Today, this traditional Reformed emphasis on Christ the *transformer* of culture (rather than Christ *against* culture) is also seen in several prominent Reformed/Presbyterian theologians. A.A. van Ruler had a great vision of the "Christianizing" or "christening" (*Christianisierung/Kerstening*) of culture. In this, he is close to Abraham Kuyper, but he moves beyond him.[23] Van Ruler's impact is visible in the new RCA confessional statement, *Our Song of Hope.*[24]

This typical Reformed concern takes on a different form in the person of Thomas F. Torrance, the renowned Scottish theologian who taught for many years at the University of Edinburgh. One of his special concerns is the relation of theology to the natural sciences and the wider world of scholarship.[25] Torrance's interest as a theologian in the natural sciences is not simply an apologetic one. It derives from his deep-felt conviction that theology cannot and must not restrict itself to the God/man relationship but must take seriously the broader knowledge of God and his relationship to the world.[26] "It is distinctive of Christian theology," Torrance maintains, "that it treats of God in his relation to the world and of God in his relation to himself, not of one without the other."[27] In other words, as Christians we cannot ignore the world because man and the universe belong together and are in their totality the object of God's providential care.

An American theological leader of this type is Herbert Richardson, a Presbyterian who formerly taught at Harvard Divinity School and is now a professor at St. Michael's College, of the University of Toronto. In his programmatic work, *Toward an American Theology,* Richardson seeks to show that in the American philosophical-theological tradition there is a distinctive perspective which provides a "rich lode for those who wish to shape the coming age." More specifically, this includes a theocratic hope and a vision of "holy worldliness, the sanctification of all things by the Holy Spirit."[28]

If this sounds a little like van Ruler, it is not a coincidence. Richardson too has been influenced by the Dutch theologian. Thus, what purports to be a peculiarly American theology converges at certain points with some distinctive Dutch Reformed emphases, and both derive from Calvin's vision of a world where God's sovereign will would be acknowledged in every sphere. Whether this vision finds its natural and logical development in a Kuyperian type of sphere-sovereignty is debatable, but there is no denying that "the hallmark of the Calvinist tradition is its development of a biblically Reformed world-and-life-view."[29] The true Calvinist, while fighting evil in all its forms—personal as well as corporate—will not rest content until "the kingdom of this world has become the kingdom of our Lord and of his Christ" (Rv 11:15).

ELEVEN

Misunderstanding Eleven

*That in the Reformed tradition the work
and reality of the Holy Spirit is ignored.*

IT IS NOT DIFFICULT to see how this misunderstanding could
arise. Both on a popular and on a more scholarly level, Scottish
Presbyterians and Dutch Calvinists have been characterized as
solid, sober, reflective Christians, hardly distinguished by the
gifts and graces of the Spirit. In contrast to Methodists (with
their traditional emphasis on experience and holiness), Baptists
(with their stress on conversion and simple biblical piety), and
Holiness and Pentecostal denominations (with their focus on
ecstatic experiences of the Holy Spirit), Reformed Christians
have been noted for their concern for pure doctrine and doing
everything "decently and in order." Almost everything that is
often associated with the work of the Holy Spirit—a warm
piety, evangelistic fervor, spontaneous testimonies, speaking in
tongues, and miraculous healings—seems to be lacking in
Reformed/Presbyterian Churches.

At least five things can be said in responding to this criticism:

1) This portrayal of typical Reformed types is, unfortunately,
often true. Whether because they hail from northern climates
and represent middle-class backgrounds or because of their
emphasis on a well-trained ministry and doctrinal preaching,
Reformed Christians do tend to be reserved about their faith. It
is probably not unfair to describe them as cool and cerebral in

contrast to the warm enthusiasm and spontaneity of Wesleyan, Baptist, and Pentecostal types.

Part of the problem may be theological. As Lewis Mudge, a Presbyterian theologian (now Dean of McCormick Theological Seminary), once observed, our creeds and confessions do not do justice to the biblical emphasis on the work of the Holy Spirit. "The result is that in reading what the Bible says about the Spirit we are blind and deaf."[1] That charge should not be limited to Reformed Christians. The church at large has been guilty on that score. Even so, there is no denying that the special gift of the Reformed tradition has been its theology, not its "saints."

2) The other side of the ledger is that the doctrine of the Holy Spirit has received special attention in the Reformed tradition, beginning with Calvin. As was pointed out earlier,[2] Calvin was not the loveless, Spirit-less dogmatician he has often been portrayed in popular caricature. He lacked the geniality and earthiness of Martin Luther, but he was not lacking in a warm, passionate piety.[3] He spoke frequently of the necessity of a sound piety,[4] and his motto was a flaming heart.

In fact, a strong case can be made for the thesis that Calvin was more a theologian of the heart than of the head. (*Heart,* however, for Calvin means not so much the seat of the emotions or affections, as in contemporary usage, but rather the existential core of the personality.) This is especially true in his understanding of faith, which is from beginning to end a work of the Holy Spirit. In his first catechism he begins his discussion of true faith in this way: "Now we are to conceive the Christian faith as no bare knowledge of God or understanding of Scripture which rattles around the brain and affects the *heart* not at all."[5] Later in the same work, he adds, "Therefore it is perfectly clear that faith is the enlightenment of the Holy Spirit by which our minds are illumined and our *hearts* confirmed in a sure persuasion within, which establishes that God's truth is so sure that He cannot but supply what He has promised to us He will do by His Holy Word."[6]

Calvin never deviated in this emphasis. In the last edition of the *Institutes*, written over twenty years later, he constantly reiterates this theme: faith requires knowledge and understanding, but it is above all a matter of the heart.[7] In his fullest, most formal definition of faith he declares, "We call it a firm and certain knowledge of God's benevolence toward us, founded upon the truth of the freely given promise in Christ, both revealed to our minds and sealed upon our *hearts* through the Holy Spirit" (III.2.7).[8] Elsewhere, even more explicitly, faith is "more of the *heart* than the brain, and more of the disposition than the understanding" (II.2.8). For "faith is much higher than human understanding. It will not be enough for the mind to be illumined by the Spirit of God unless the *heart* is also strengthened and supported by his power" (III.2.33).

One could add many other illustrations to show why leading scholars have come to the conclusion that Calvin, more than any of the other reformers, was the "theologian of the Holy Spirit."[9] Space limitations do not permit an elaboration of this thesis except to point briefly to some other areas where the Holy Spirit plays a prominent role in Calvin's theology.[10]

In his stress on the sovereignty and freedom of God, Calvin never tires of pointing out that our whole existence is the result of the gracious work of God's Spirit. The Christian life originates in and is continually renewed by the grace and power of the Spirit (III.1.3-4). At the same time, the Spirit is at work in a more general way in the world, preserving, restoring, and guiding. "It is the Spirit who, everywhere diffused, sustains all things, causes them to grow, and quickens them in heaven and earth" (I.13.14). All that is good, true, and beautiful in the world—even among pagans and atheists—is ultimately due to the Spirit of God (II.2.12-20).

Calvin's most original contribution to the evangelical understanding of the nature and the authority of scripture was his doctrine of the internal witness or testimony of the Holy Spirit. According to Calvin, neither the written Word nor the proclaimed Word has any power or persuasion apart from the secret working and witness of the Spirit (I.7.4-5; I.9.1-3).[11]

Returning to the Christian life, it is significant that the key category Calvin uses here is that of regeneration.[12] "Faith flows from regeneration," as well as "newness of life and other gifts of the Holy Spirit" (Commentary on John, 1.13). We have already seen how he relates faith to the work of the Spirit. One thing further should be noted: his beautiful doctrine of the mystical faith-union of the believer with his Lord.[13] "We hold ourselves to be united with Christ by the secret power of his Spirit" (III.11.5).[14]

Moreover, Calvin, no less than Wesley and the Pentecostals,[15] was concerned about sanctification. Whereas, in terms of accent, Luther could be called the theologian of justification, Calvin might well be labeled the theologian of sanctification.[16] Often Calvin speaks of "the leading of the Spirit," an aspect of Calvin's thought that has not received the attention it deserves.[17] Hendrikus Berkhof maintains that "the famous third book of the *Institutes* ["The Way in Which We Receive the Grace of Christ"] contains great riches in the field of pneumatology, many of which have not yet been uncovered by Reformed churches."[18]

Others, however, would point to Calvin's doctrine of the church and sacraments as the sphere in which the role of the Holy Spirit comes to the fore. Calvin was a high churchman in the sense that he had no hesitancy in repeating the famous phrase of the early church father, Cyprian: "For those to whom God is Father the Church may also be Mother" (IV.1.1.). He could say this because he was convinced that the church is "a union of Head (Christ) and members (believers) in love and the Spirit."[19] For Calvin, the church is a living organism in which there is a dynamic interplay between Christ, the head, and his members, the body.[20] Calvin's view of the church has been described as a "pneumatocracy," i.e., as the sphere where the Holy Spirit rules.[21]

The role of the Spirit in Calvin's doctrine of the sacraments is equally prominent. At almost every crucial point in a discussion, whether of baptism or the Lord's Supper, Calvin brings in the Holy Spirit. For it is "he who brings the grace of God with him, gives a place for the sacraments among us, and makes them bear fruit." The sacraments may be "visible signs" of God's grace manifest to us in Christ, but they have no efficacy unless God works in us "by invisible grace through the Holy Spirit" (IV.14.18).[22]

3. Although the above is hardly more than a summary, it should amply illustrate that Calvin did not, indeed, ignore the Holy Spirit. But what about his successors? Did this lively and pervasive sense of the work of the Holy Spirit die out in later generations? To some extent, this was the case in the period of Orthodoxy in the seventeenth century. The reaction of pietism also lacked the balance of Calvin. These two movements were followed in the eighteenth and nineteenth centuries by a liberalism which talked much about "spirit" but which knew little of the biblical understanding of the Holy Spirit.[23]

However, within the Reformed fold, there are some notable exceptions. In the Netherlands in the seventeenth century, there developed an experiential theology which emphasized the new birth, a personal knowledge of Christ's saving grace and sanctification.[24] Out of this movement came one of the first great evangelists in the United States, German-born Theodorus Jacobus Frelinghuysen (1691-1747).[25] He served the latter part of his career a Reformed Church minister in New Jersey. Gilbert Tennent, the Presbyterian revivalist, was influenced by Frelinghuysen, as were the leaders of the Great Awakening, Jonathan Edwards and George Whitefield. All of them were Calvinists of a sort, and all were charismatic figures, if one uses the word in a non-Pentecostal sense.

Further evidence that the Holy Spirit was not overlooked in succeeding centuries is seen in the many Presbyterian Puritan pastors and theologians in nineteenth century Scotland who produced major works on the person and work of the Holy Spirit.[26] In more modern times, Reformed theologians in the Netherlands have shown a special interest in the doctrine of the Holy Spirit. The classic in this field is Abraham Kuyper's monumental popular work, *The Work of the Holy Spirit*, completed in 1888 and published in the United States in 1900.[27]

This interest in the Holy Spirit by Dutch theologians has continued down to the present. Mention has already been made of Hendrikus Berkhof's work. Less well known is the late O. Noordmans, whose popular meditations on the Holy Spirit were translated into German.[28] There is also A.A. van Ruler, who is considered the theologian of the Holy Spirit, par excellence.[29]

Little has been written by Scottish Presbyterians about the Holy Spirit recently but, until the flurry of interest in the Holy Spirit due to the charismatic movement, two of the best serious theological studies were by American Presbyterians: George S. Hendry's *The Holy Spirit in Christian Theology,*[30] and Arnold Come's *Human Spirit and Holy Spirit.*[31]

4) At this juncture, I can imagine that some readers will still be unconvinced. All this impressive literature notwithstanding, there may still be a solid basis for the misunderstanding. Calvin may have done justice to the Holy Spirit. So also a number of Reformed pietists, Puritans, and theologians in succeeding centuries. The fact remains that typical Reformed/Presbyterian Christians, past or present, are hardly distinguished by their practical knowledge and experience of the power of the Spirit, especially as manifested in his extraordinary gifts.

This criticism may be based on a misunderstanding of the nature of the work of the Spirit. I will say more about that later. But for now, let us consider the phenomenon of the neo-Pentecostal or charismatic movement from a Reformed perspective. Many from both sides have assumed that they are mutually exclusive, if not antithetical.

The Reformed reformers—Zwingli, Calvin, and Knox—had little interest in the gifts of the Spirit. They apparently assumed that the so-called "extraordinary" gifts such as prophesying, healing, and speaking in tongues were temporary and no longer relevant.[32] In the modern period, the notion that such gifts ceased in the apostolic period became accepted dogma in orthodox Presbyterian/Reformed circles. B.B. Warfield expended considerable effort to prove that miracles ceased with the apostles. Warfield, a brilliant biblical and theological scholar, is still highly esteemed in conservative Presbyterian circles.[33] He published *Counterfeit Miracles* in 1918, subsequently reprinted under the title *Miracles: Yesterday and Today, Real and Counterfeit* (Grand Rapids, Mich.: Eerdmans, 1965). His thesis is that whereas it was quite appropriate for the apostolic church to be "a miracle-working church," spiritual gifts (*charismata*) of a miraculous kind "necessarily passed away with [the apostolic church]."[34]

Some people will be astounded to discover that such a view has prevailed in Presbyterian/Reformed Churches for over a half a century. It should be added immediately that this view is still being defended today by able and respected Reformed and Presbyterian scholars such as Anthony Hoekema,[35] emeritus professor of systematic theology at Calvin Seminary in Grand Rapids, and Richard Gaffin, Jr.,[36] professor of New Testament at Westminster Seminary in Philadelphia. The explanation for the recent flurry of speaking in tongues (glossolalia) "after 1800 years of virtual silence" is to be explained psychologically, maintains Hoekema. "Glossolalia as we see it today is for the most part neither directly inspired by the Spirit nor directly induced by demons, but is a human reaction which has been psychologically induced."[37] Gaffin's line of argumentation is more biblically oriented than Hoekema's, but his conclusions are basically the same: "Tongues are withdrawn from the life of the church along with prophecy and whatever other foundational gifts are bound up with the presence of the apostolate in the church."[38]

This is definitely a minority view. Few New Testament scholars and theologians, whatever their denominational background or theological inclination, believe that speaking in tongues, prophesying, and healings can all be explained psychologically, or that they are spurious or even a work of the devil, as is occasionally alleged.

In any case, beginning about thirty years ago, leading Reformed/Presbyterian Church leaders and theologians have increasingly acknowledged the validity and importance of the Pentecostal—and especially the more recent charismatic or neo-Pentecostal—movement. I still recall the shock I experienced in reading an article by Henry Van Dusen, the liberal Presbyterian who was then president of Union Seminary in New York. He related his very positive impressions of the Pentecostal movement as he experienced it on a recent trip to the Caribbean Islands. His discovery of the vitality of the 8.5 million Pentecostals there led him to speak of them as representing "a new reformation" and a new, powerful "third force in Christendom."[39]

A little earlier (1953), the well-known Scottish Presbyterian missionary theologian, Lesslie Newbigin, acknowledged the importance and contributions of the Pentecostal movement.[40] It is especially significant that the conservative Dutch Reformed theologian G.C. Berkouwer by 1950 quite apart from much experience of or contact with Pentecostals came to the conclusion on theological grounds that miracles can and do indeed occur today.

> He who sees the miracles of Holy Scripture inseparably connected with the saving and redeeming activity of God knows that there can be no talk of a decrease or diminishing of the power of God unto salvation in this world. . . . He who thinks that . . . miracles no longer can occur may seriously ask himself whether he thinks in terms of God's power over the world or from a secret capitulation to determinism.[41]

Berkouwer's countryman Hendrikus Berkhof was even more explicit. He notes that "pneumatology [the doctrine of the Holy Spirit] is a neglected field of systematic theology.[42] He points out that part of the difficulty is the bad experience the traditional churches have had throughout history with Spirit movements—from the Montanists in the second century to the Anabaptists and Quakers in the sixteenth century, and the Pentecostals at the beginning of our century. Words like enthusiasts, spiritualists, faith healers, etc., usually evoke negative emotions among most Protestants. The result is an unhappy and sterile alternative.

> On the one hand, we see the established larger churches which are unwilling to focus their attention on the action of the Holy Spirit; in their midst faith is in danger of becoming something intellectual, traditional and institutional. On the other hand, we see the rapidly increasing Pentecostal movements, where the reality of the Spirit is often sought in the emotional, individualistic, and extravagant. Both parts live by the lacks and mistakes of the other, which give them a good pretext not to see their own lacks and mistakes, or the biblical truth represented by the other.[43]

He feels that the revivalists and Pentecostals may well be correct in challenging our traditional analysis of regeneration as having only two aspects: justification and sanctification. They refer to a third aspect, that of the baptism or filling of the Spirit. Berkhof challenges the usual Pentecostal exegesis here, but he attempts to break through the "watertight partition-wall between these two groups," because this partition is a detriment to both parties.[44]

On the American scene, the most significant development from a Presbyterian/Reformed standpoint was the appointment by the 180th General Assembly (1968) of the United Presbyterian Church of a special committee on the work of the Holy Spirit. This was in response to various overtures for study of the Holy Spirit with special reference to glossolalia and other charismatic gifts occurring in the United Presbyterian Church. The results of this study were published in 1970 by the General Assembly under the title *The Work of the Holy Spirit.*[45] The report is relatively brief (56 pages), but is remarkably thorough, irenic, and pastoral. The committee members utilized the reports of subcommittees on exegesis, theology, psychology, and healing, as well as correspondence with non-Presbyterians. They also personally interviewed "those with both positive and negative experience of charismatic phenomena both within and outside the United Presbyterian Church."[46]

Of the various conclusions which the committee reached I find three to be of special interest:

a) Concerning the view that supernatural gifts or miracles ceased with the death of the apostles, the committee concludes that "it is difficult to validate this view either exegetically or historically." At the same time, they urge us to "test the spirits to see whether they are of God" (1 Jn 4:1), and recognize "that each of the authentic gifts of the Spirit has had its counterfeits and frauds."[47]

b) Concerning the allegation that most, if not all, Pentecostal experiences can be explained (away) psychologically, the committee concurs with the judgment of Fr. Edward O'Connor, a theologian with extensive experience among Catholic Pentecostals. He holds that "the [Pentecostal] experience is not produced by emotion, it does not consist in emotion, and its chief and characteristic effects are not emotional."[48]

c) Concerning speaking in tongues, the committee simply presented a summary of Paul's argument in 1 Corinthians 12-14: "Speaking in tongues can be good, but prophesying in intelligible speech for the edification of the congregation is better (1 Cor 14:5), and the love for God and men is best of all (1 Cor 12:31; 13:13)."[49]

There is, however, one fundamental biblical-theological problem that divides Pentecostalism, as traditionally taught, and the Reformed tradition: the so-called "baptism in/of the Holy Spirit." In Pentecostal theology this experience is subsequent to and distinct from becoming a Christian. According to this way of thinking, two Spirit-baptisms are normal for Christians: the first when one is baptized, the second when one receives "the benefits of a permanent, personal, and full indwelling of the Spirit . . . providing power for Christian service, particularly evangelistic service, with the equipment of the spiritual gifts."[50]

Reformed theologians are quick to point out that the expression, "baptism in the Holy Spirit," is not found in the New Testament. Moreover, in response to the Pentecostal claim that the *idea* is biblical even if the precise phrase is not, Reformed theologians reply that this idea or doctrine is also foreign to the New Testament teaching about the Holy Spirit. In one sense, we must be filled with the Spirit again and again, they would maintain. But also, there is only one baptism (Eph 4:5) and one gift of the Spirit which is to be identified with becoming a Christian.[51]

This theological difference, however, is not insuperable. Evidence of this is seen in the fact that large numbers of neo-Pentecostals (or charismatics) are to be found among Roman Catholic, Episcopalian, Lutheran, Methodist, and Presbyterian denominations. Most of them have not forsaken their particular theological traditions. Although not as large as some other fellowships, Presbyterian charismatics have become so numerous that they have their own organization and publication.[52]

5) Finally, and briefly, it must be noted that this misunderstanding is based on a misunderstanding of the biblical view of the nature and work of the Holy Spirit. The popular understanding of the nature of the Spirit's activity, especially in Holiness and Pentecostal circles, is often narrow and one-sided. To identify the Holy Spirit only with sudden and dramatic experiences—whether radical conversions, instantaneous Christian perfection, miraculous healings, or ecstatic utterances—does not do justice to the variety and scope of the Spirit's ways and work. The work of the Spirit in creation and preservation, in reason and conscience, regeneration and sanctification, the church and its mission, culture and history is frequently neglected in presentations of the work of the Spirit. The Spirit of God moves quietly, corporately, and cosmically as well as dramatically and individually. Before one criticizes Reformed Christians of lacking the Spirit,[53] one should note *all* that the Bible has to say about the Spirit. Above all, one should not emphasize the *gifts* of the Spirit (1 Cor 12:28-31; Rom 12:6-8) to the exclusion of the *fruit* of the Spirit (Gal 5:22-23).[54]

It might not be an either/or situation: that is, dramatic experiences of speaking in tongues and prophesying as opposed to quiet dedication and the growth of a Spirit-filled life. Unfortunately, biblical balance is often lacking in the Christian life. Pentecostal types tend to focus on the "individual/spontaneous" aspects of the Spirit's work, while traditionalists stress the "continuing/collective" experience of the Spirit.[55] Or, to express the contrast in biblical terms, Pentecostals and charismatics revel in the *freedom* given by the Spirit (2 Cor 3:17), whereas Presbyterians traditionally appeal to *order* (1 Cor 14:40). Both are important and necessary but often exist in tension.[56]

A frequent Reformed complaint about charismatics and pietists is their tendency to make experience their norm. Reformed theologians point out that our norm and authority should not be experience but the Word. They accordingly produce impressive theological treatises. To this many Baptists, Wesleyans, and Pentecostals might well reply: "So you have the theology; but we have the Spirit!" To this I would reply "yes and no." It is true that we have often been lacking in a vital experience of the joy and freedom of the Spirit. But these other traditions have often shown little appreciation for other aspects of the Spirit's work. We can learn from each other, both doctrinally and experientially.[57] No group, including the Pentecostals, has a corner on the Spirit. All of us can well repeat the ancient prayer, *"Veni Creator Spiritus!"* ("Come, Creator Spirit!").

TWELVE

Misunderstanding Twelve

*That to be Reformed is to be anti-ecumenical
and frequently schismatic.*

A SUPERFICIAL READING of relatively recent church history
might seem to provide considerable ammunition for this
charge. The Reformed Church in the Netherlands and the
Presbyterian Church in Scotland both experienced serious
disruptions and divisions in the nineteenth century. (There
were two secessions from the Church of Scotland already in the
eighteenth century.) Some of those divisions were transplanted
to the New World by emigrants. These American Reformed
and Presbyterian Churches were later plagued by further splits.
Out of the Reformed Church in America came the Christian
Reformed Church, and from that denomination the Protestant
Reformed Church. Out of the main American Presbyterian
Church came the Presbyterian Church U.S. (Southern), the
Cumberland Presbyterian Church, the Orthodox Presbyterian
Church, and, out of this last, the Bible Presbyterian Church,
which has subsequently split into two factions. (This list of
schisms and splits in the Reformed/Presbyterian family is not
exhaustive. For example, the Reformed Presbyterian Church, a
group of about 20,000 members that sings only psalms and uses
no instrumental accompaniment, claims unbroken descent
from the Scottish Covenanters.)

Thus, the story of Presbyterian and Reformed Churches,
especially in North America, is not a very happy one from the

standpoint of the unity of the church. Moreover, one of the leading apostles of schism in the United States is Carl McIntyre, leader of the Bible Presbyterian Church and the International Council of Churches. One of the causes of all this divisiveness is the fact that Reformed Christians take doctrine so seriously. As a result, what would look like a minor doctrinal deviation to outsiders can rather easily lead to a split in one of the churches in the Presbyterian/Reformed family.

At the same time it should be noted that there have been several reunions in the last quarter century. The Presbyterian Church of North America and the United Presbyterian Church joined forces in 1958. This denomination, the United Presbyterian Church U.S.A., and the next largest Presbyterian body, the Presbyterian Church U.S., decided to reunite in 1983. Two splinter groups—the Presbyterian Church in America and the Reformed Presbyterian Church, Evangelical Synod—agreed to become one at their respective national assemblies in June 1982. There is also the case of the Reformed Church in the United States (German) which united with the Evangelical Synod of North America in 1934 to form the Evangelical and Reformed Church. This group in turn united with the Congregational Christian Church in 1957 to form the United Church of Christ. Thus, the record of late is considerably better, although the Reformed Church in America and the Christian Reformed Church seem only mildly interested in each other and even less interested in anyone else.[1]

However, this is only one side of the picture. The track record of Baptists and Lutherans is little or no better, so it would be quite erroneous to conclude that Reformed Christians have a corner on division and disunity. More important, from the time of the Reformation until the present, many of the strongest and ablest proponents of the unity and catholicity of the church have come from the Presbyterian/Reformed tradition. John Calvin hated schism and was one of the most zealous promoters of unity among the Protestant forces in the sixteenth century. The earliest Reformed confessions speak forcefully about the catholic (i.e., universal) nature of the church. When the ecumenical tide began to rise in the nineteenth century, one of the first leaders was Alexander Duff, a Scottish Presbyterian missionary to India. Throughout most of the brief history of the World Council of Churches its leadership has been Reformed: the first General Secretary, W.A. Visser 't Hooft, was Dutch Reformed, and his successor, Eugene Carson Blake, was an American United Presbyterian. Other figures from our tradition who have played leading roles in the World Council of Churches are Hendrik Kraemer, Lesslie Newbigin, John Mackay, and Albert Van den Heuvel, to mention only a few of the more prominent leaders.

There is an ambivalence in Reformed/Presbyterian history. On the one hand, there is a firm commitment to the unity of the church in the sixteenth century and a distinctive contribution to the ecumenical movement in the twentieth. On the other hand, Presbyterian and Reformed Christians are noted for their fierce doctrinal controversies and frequent divisions.

Perhaps these are the major and minor motifs in our history. The former president of Princeton Seminary, John Mackay, is convinced that among Presbyterians there is a classical commitment to the church universal and the injunction to cultivate the unity of the church. However, "the mainstream of Presbyterian witness has been shadowed by a type of sectarian Presbyterianism which . . . has been schismatic, sometimes even glorying in schism as the clearest evidence of loyalty to Christ."[2]

Perhaps there is a paradox or contradiction within the Reformed tradition. Herman Harmelink III is convinced that this is the case with the Reformed Church in America. He explores the reasons for the contradiction in the life of the Reformed Church, "by which she has exhibited genuine interest in and concern for Christian unity but great hesitancy about church union."[3]

There are various reasons for this ambivalence or contradiction, some justifiable, or at least understandable, others foolish and sinful. In the former category would be concern for purity of doctrine and the fear of certain types of bureaucracies. In the latter category would be ethnocentrism and fear of being swallowed up by a larger denomination. Frequently, the real reasons for opposing church union by certain Reformed Church members have been non-theological, despite protestations to the contrary. On the other side, there have been those who seemed to favor church union just for the sake of union, no matter what the cost theologically or ecclesiastically. It should be noted in passing that a concern for the *unity* of the church does not necessarily require commitment to every proposed church *union*. Sometimes just the opposite may be the case.

Here again, we may gain perspective and insight by going back to the sources of our tradition. Calvin did everything in his power to foster the unity of the church. But he was no "ecumaniac" ready for unity at any price. The following two passages from his commentary on John's Gospel accurately reflect his viewpoint.

> Schism is the worst and most harmful evil in the Church of God . . . It is those who will not be obedient to the truth of God who tear the church by schism. Yet, better that men should disagree, than that they should all with one consent secede from godliness (*Commentary*, 9:16).[4]

> It is for us to work hard and strive in every way to bring if possible the whole world to agree in the unity of the faith. (*Commentary*, 10:8).[5]

Here we have three criteria for true unity: obedience to the truth, genuine godliness or piety, and unity of faith. However, there is still the practical problem as to how to determine what is essential and nonessential regarding truth or the faith. The classic Protestant definition of a true church is one in which the Word of God is faithfully proclaimed and the sacraments are properly administered.[6] But this still leaves us with the question as to when we have the "true" or "pure" ministry of Word and sacraments.[7] Everything hinges on how one defines truth and purity.

Calvin warns against overscrupulousness in regard to doctrinal and ethical standards. A church, says Calvin, may "swarm with many faults" (IV.1.12). It may, like the Church in Corinth, have serious defects in the administration of the Lord's Supper, discipline, moral tone, and the understanding of the gospel itself. But if the fundamental teachings concerning God and Christ are still sound, a true church exists. Moreover, there is no justification for leaving such a church despite all its errors, if it does not meet our standards. Perfectionism is unbiblical whether it is applied to personal sanctity or the life of a church. As Calvin sharply warns (*Commentary on 1 Corinthians,* 1:2):

> It is a dangerous temptation to think there is no church where perfect purity is lacking. Anyone who is obsessed by that idea must cut himself off from everybody else, and appear to himself to be the only saint in the world, or he must set up a sect of his own along with other hypocrites.

How much, then, is it necessary to believe in order to avoid heresy on the one hand and perfectionism on the other? Calvin distinguishes between essential and nonessential matters of faith. In the latter case, "a difference of opinion . . . should in nowise be the basis of schism among Christians." For the former, characteristic essential doctrines are "God is one; Christ is God and the Son of God; our salvation rests on God's mercy and the like" (IV.1.12). The one fundamental doctrine "which it is forbidden to overthrow, is that we might learn Christ. For Christ is the one and only foundation of the Church" (*Commentary on 1 Corinthians,* 3:11). In other words, the final test of whether a church is a true church is its doctrine of Christ. Everything hinges on the question "What do you think of the Christ?" (Mt 22:42).

Calvin practiced what he preached. He not only taught and wrote about the unity of the church, he also worked hard at it. Throughout his life he sought to promote understanding and unity among the warring Lutheran and Zwinglian (German Reformed) factions. Like his friend and one time mentor Bucer he was amazingly irenic and diplomatic in sensitive ecumenical negotiations and was quite willing to compromise when it came to nonessential matters of the faith. Early in his career (1540 and 1541), he attended conferences where Lutherans and Roman Catholics discussed the possibility of reunion. He was also very appreciative and conciliatory in his relations to Luther (whom he never met) and his followers.[8] One has to marvel at his friendship with and loyalty to Melanchthon, Luther's colleague and principal theologian, for Melanchthon was notoriously unstable and held several views quite different from Calvin's.

Within Switzerland, Calvin was the principal figure in working out a union of the disparate Protestant Swiss factions. After almost ten years of negotiations, a basis for union, the famous *Consensus Tigurinus* (*Zurich Consensus*, 1549) was achieved. It all started when Calvin wrote to Bullinger (Zwingli's successor and the leader of the German-Swiss Reformed Churches):

> What, my dear Bullinger, should more concern us in writing at this time, than to keep up and strengthen brotherly friendship between us by all possible means? We see how much it concerns not our church alone but all Christianity that all to whom the Lord has entrusted any charge in his church should agree in true concord. . . . We must therefore purposefully and carefully cherish association and friendship with all true ministers of Christ . . . in order that the churches to which we minister the Word of God may faithfully agree together. As for me, as afar as in me lies, I will always labor to this end.[9]

After the opening of the Council of Trent, Calvin became even more active in his quest for a united Protestantism.[10] No doubt, one of his motives was a pragmatic one. If Protestants were to hold their own over against a revitalized Roman Catholicism, a united front was highly desirable. In 1557, he tried to persuade Melanchthon to arrange for a conference in Germany on behalf of peace and union. In 1560, he made further attempts to renew this union project and now proposed the assembling of "a free and universal council to put an end to the divisions of Christendom.[11] The next year, he even gave his consent to holding a colloquy at Poissy with Roman Catholics and would have attended himself had not his friends prevented him. This is all the more remarkable in that his frail body was being wracked by ever more frequent bouts of the painful illness which was to bring him to his death only three years later.

One of the most eloquent testimonies to Calvin's zeal for the unity of the church is his famous letter to Archbishop Cranmer in England. Earlier (1552), Cranmer had invited Calvin, Melanchthon, Bullinger, and others to a meeting in Lambeth Palace for the purpose of devising a creed suitable to all Reformed Churches. This proposal came to naught because of the death of Edward VI and the martyrdom of Cranmer. But Calvin's reply to Cranmer is moving.

> I wish indeed it could be brought about that men of learning and authority from the different Churches might meet somewhere and, after thoroughly discussing the different articles of faith, should, by a unanimous decision, hand down to posterity some certain rule of faith. . . . As to myself, if I should be thought of any use, I would not, if need be, object to cross ten seas for such a purpose. If the assisting of England were alone concerned, that would be motive enough for me. Much more, therefore, am I of opinion that I ought to grudge no labour or trouble, seeing that the object in view is an agreement among the learned, to be drawn up by the weight of their authority according to Scripture, in order to unite widely severed Churches.[12]

Calvin, as A. Mitchell Hunter has observed, "was mastered by the vision of a world-wide Church one in Christ, and he regarded it as one of the great ends of his earthly mission to promote its realization."[13] This vision, as we have seen, was not his alone but was shared by several other sixteenth-century reformers with varying degrees of enthusiasm.

The catholicity of the Church of Jesus Christ also finds expression in many of the early Reformed confessions. One of the finest expressions of this conviction is found in Article 27 of the *Belgic Confession*:

> We believe and profess one unique catholic or universal Church, which is a holy gathering of true believers in Christ.
> . . . This holy Church, moreover, is not confined, bound or limited to a certain place or to certain persons, but is spread and scattered over the whole world; and yet is joined and united with heart and will in one and the same Spirit and power.[14]

The *Westminster Confession* speaks in similar terms of the church (in XXV.1-6) and then, in reference to the communion of saints, adds the significant phrase: "Which communion, as God offereth opportunity, is to be extended unto all those who in every place call upon the name of the Lord Jesus" (XX.VI.2). John Mackay, after quoting this phrase, asks, "Could there be a more decisive testimony to what it means, in a practical sense, to belong to the Holy Catholic Church or a more articulate clarion call to intercommunion?"[15]

Twentieth-century heirs of this great tradition have a long way to go to recover the riches of what was realized in the sixteenth and seventeenth centuries. Our fathers knew that to be truly reformed we must also be catholic as well as evangelical.

THIRTEEN

On Being Reformed

Some Characteristic and Distinctive Emphases

WHILE NOTING some special emphases in the Reformed tradition, it is important to keep in mind that this tradition is only a part of the larger tradition of the historic Christian faith. Reformed Churches are members of the one, holy, catholic church. For the most part, our beliefs are the same as evangelical Christians in all times and in all parts of the world. Accordingly, in regard to the fundamental doctrines of the Christian faith we can make no special claims.[1] On the contrary, we are indebted not only to the reformers but also to the ancient fathers of the church for the great Christian heritage which is ours today.

All this notwithstanding, we are also children of the Reformation with its recovery of certain evangelical themes: the Word alone, by grace alone, and by faith alone. More particularly, we are a part of a specific Reformation tradition known as Reformed or Presbyterian. Although many in this tradition call themselves "Calvinists," others do not rally around the five points of Calvinism: total depravity, unconditional election, limited atonement, irresistible grace, and the perseverance of the saints (often referred to by the acronym TULIP). These so-called points do not come from Calvin but from the *Canons of Dort,* which were composed in the Netherlands over fifty years after Calvin's death. The Reformed tradition does not stem from Calvin alone. Before him there were other Reformed reformers—Zwingli, Bucer, Oecolampadius, and Farel, to name only a few—and there were others who worked with him or were indebted to him such as Bullinger, Knox, and Beza.

Yet, despite all this diversity, which is with us in even greater measure today, there are a number of doctrinal emphases which are especially characteristic of the Reformed tradition. However, in order to capture the spirit of the Reformed tradition, it is also necessary to see that there is a Reformed piety, ethos, and approach to the world which distinguishes it from other traditions. I can only suggest a few of these characteristics.

God-Centered

The most fundamental and comprehensive thing that can be said about the Reformed tradition is that it is theocentric or God-centered. In a sense, this is true of all Christians, but, in contrast to Pelagianism and Arminianism,* the Calvinist affirms that man's will is *not* free and that man does *not* take the initiative in response to the redemption offered in Jesus Christ. Moreover, in contrast to certain types of evangelicalism, the Reformed Christian focuses on God, not on his own experience. It is not *my* conversion, *my* faith, or *my* good life that counts in the last analysis. *God's* goodness and grace and *God's* sovereign will are the bedrock of my salvation. This is why "in a particularly profound sense Calvinism is theocentric theology. For the Calvinist the doctrine of God is the doctrine of doctrines, in a sense the only doctrine."[2]

Granted, in the Bible we have passages which speak both of God's almighty power and man's responsibility, God's election and man's decision. The Calvinist does not wish to deny the latter part of these correlations, but the accent is characteristically placed on God's sovereign grace. Hence, in Reformed

---

*Pelagianism denies original sin and interprets sin as a deliberate choice of evil by a will which is free to choose either good or evil. This view is attributed to Pelagius, a fourth-century Briton who was a foe of the great church father, Augustine. We have already discussed Arminianism.

circles, one hears frequently about the sovereignty and providence of God, election, and predestination. The Arminian will stress, "work out your own salvation with fear and trembling" (Phil 2:12b). The Calvinist will respond that this is only possible because "God is at work in you, both to will and to work for his good pleasure" (Phil 2:13).

To express the paradox in the beautiful words of a hymn that ought to be a favorite in Reformed and Presbyterian Churches:

> I sought the Lord, and afterward I knew
> He moved my soul to seek Him, seeking me;
> It was not I that found, O Saviour true;
> No, I was found of Thee.[3]

In short, when we believe, it is very much a human act and decision. But faith is at the same time a gift. "For by grace you have been saved through faith; and this is not your own doing, it is the gift of God . . ." (Eph 2:8). This in turn is also the work of the Spirit. It is not even possible to confess " 'Jesus is Lord' except by the Holy Spirit" (1 Cor 12:3). As far as the life of faith is concerned, "there is no drop of vigor in us save what the Holy Spirit instills" (II.15.1).

Calvinism is Augustinianism, an exaltation of the sovereign grace of God. In effect the five points of Calvinism are all about *grace*. The terminology may not be the most felicitous (e.g., "total depravity" and "limited atonement"), but these five points are "not five separate doctrines that we assert almost as disjointed elements, but rather articulation of one point which is the grace of God."[4]

The baptism of a child, in the context of God's covenant of grace, is one of the most striking illustrations of this grace. The objection of opponents to infant baptism is that the child does nothing. Precisely! Both the present state and future fate of that child depend not so much on the child's or the parents' faith and fidelity (though they cannot be discounted) as on God's sovereign grace. "The gospel begins with the foolishness of baptism,"[5] for "the baptism of a helpless child was [to

Reformed believers] the most dramatic and precious symbol of God's freely given grace."[6]

As Calvin observes in regard to the phrase in Ephesians 2:5 ("By grace you have been saved . . ."), Paul "is never satisfied with proclaiming the richness of grace, and accordingly emphasizes the same thing with many words, that everything in our salvation might be ascribed to God" (*Commentary*). Or as the *Heidelberg Catechism* puts it, true faith is

> not only a certain knowledge by which I accept as true all that God has revealed to us in his Word, but also a wholehearted trust which the Holy Spirit creates in me through the gospel, that, not only to others, but to me also God has given the forgiveness of sins, everlasting righteousness and salvation, *out of sheer grace* solely for the sake of Christ's saving work. (Q. 21, emphasis mine)

One thing must be added. God's soverign grace is not simply an individual thing that affects only me and my salvation. The sovereignty of God has cosmic dimensions. His sovereign will is working itself out in the farthest reaches of the universe, and in time and eternity. The Reformed outlook is one of great scope and grandeur. It stresses the power of God manifest not only in creation, preservation, and providential ruling but above all as it is seen in the resurrection and ascension of Jesus Christ. He is the "King of kings and the Lord of lords" (Rv 19:16; cf. 17:14), whose kingdom shall have no end (Lk 1:33). He shall reign until "the kingdoms of the world have become the kingdom of our Lord and of his Christ" (Rv 11:15).

The sovereignty of God and of his grace comes to a focus in the lordship of Jesus Christ. As Calvin summarizes the kingly offices of Christ, "The Father has given all power to the Son that by the Son's hand he may govern, nourish, and sustain us, keep us in his care, and help us. . . . Scripture usually calls Christ 'Lord' because the Father set Christ over us to exercise his dominion through his Son" (II.15.5).

To be God-centered is thus to be Christ-centered and, as we

shall see, Spirit-centered as well. To say that Reformed theology has a theocentric thrust is simply to say that it is thoroughly trinitarian.

A People of the Word

Although *sola scripture* (by scripture alone) was a strong theme in the whole Reformation, it is in the Reformed tradition that scripture receives special prominence. A comparison of Reformed and Lutheran confessions bears this out. Lutherans tend to place the emphasis on the *material principle* of the Reformation, namely, justification by faith, whereas Reformed confessions are more interested in the *formal principle,* namely, the authority of scripture.

The earliest and most influential Lutheran confession (*Augsburg,* 1530), for example, has no section on scripture, whereas most of the Reformed confessions devote one or more paragraphs to this point very early in the confessions. The first section of the *Genevan Confession* (1536), entitled "The Lord's Work," begins: "First, we declare that we wish to follow Scripture alone as the rule of our faith and religion. . . ." (Cochrane, p. 120). The *Gallican Confession* (1559), the *Belgic Confession* (1561), the *Second Helvetic Confession* (1566), and the *Westminster Confession* (1646) all stress the authority and sole sufficiency of scripture.[7]

How do these Reformed confessions define the nature and scope of the inspiration and authority of scripture? First, it should be noted that there is no real theory of inspiration. Later Calvinists developed theories of verbal inspiration (Charles Hodge and B.B. Warfield) and plenary inspiration (Albertus Pieters), but neither Calvin nor our confessions are explicit concerning this question. Some Calvin scholars affirm that Calvin not only held to a view of verbal inspiration but that he also believed in a form of the dictation theory of inspiration (R. Seeberg, B.B. Warfield, A.M. Hunter, E.A. Dowey), whereas almost as many scholars deny this (Doumergue, Heppe, and J.K.S. Reid).

The important thing is not the *theory* of inspiration but the sufficiency and reliability of the scriptures. Here the confessions are clear. The *Gallican Confession,* which most clearly reflects Calvin's influence, speaks of the Bible as "the sure rule of our faith" and "the rule of all truth, containing all that is necessary for the service of God and for our salvation" (Articles IV and V). The *Belgic Confession* is similar but somewhat more explicit. "We believe that this Holy Scripture fully contains the will of God and that whatever man ought to believe for salvation is sufficiently taught therein." Moreover its teaching (or doctrine) is "most perfect and in every respect complete" (Article 7). The *Westminster Confession,* which often reflects the influence of scholasticism, says no more than this.

Interestingly, in view of the current debate about the *inerrancy* over against the *infallibility* of the scriptures in evangelical circles, the former words appears nowhere and the latter word rarely. The *Belgic Confession* speaks of the "infallible rule" of the scriptures (Article VII) but does not spell out the nature and scope of this infallibility. The *Westminster Confession* refers to the "infallible truth" of the scriptures but also does not develop this concept.

Where the Reformed confessions—and Calvin—are explicit is in connection with the nature of the authority of the Word. In Calvin's classic discussion of this theme in the *Institutes,* he makes one of his most distinctive contributions to Christian theology, namely, the doctrine of the inner witness of the Holy Spirit to the truth and authority of scripture. As Calvin approaches the whole question of scripture, his first concern is "not only to prepare our hearts to reverence it, but to banish all doubt." For "the Scriptures obtain full authority among believers only when men regard them as having sprung from heaven, as if there the living words of God were heard" (I.7.1). In other words, we will not believe the message of scripture "until we are persuaded beyond doubt that God is its author" (I.7.4).

Now the crucial question: How can we know for sure that the

Bible is indeed the Word of God? The scriptures contain within themselves many indications of their divine origin—their antiquity, miraculous preservation, miracles, fulfilled prophecies, and the "heavenly majesty" of the gospel message. Impressive and helpful though these evidences may be, they can never be more than "secondary aids to our feebleness" (I.7.13). Only God can provide us with the certainty we seek and require. "If we desire to provide in the best way for our consciences—that they may not be perpetually beset by the instability of doubt or vacillation, and that they may not also boggle at the smallest quibbles—we ought to seek our conviction in a higher place than human reasons, judgments, or conjectures, that is, in the secret testimony of the Spirit" (I.7.4).

This is Calvin's great contribution to the question of the authority of the scripture. Fortunately, this insight is preserved and faithfully reflected in our confessions. The *Belgic Confession* says that "we believe without any doubt all that is contained" in the scriptures, "not so much because the Church receives and approves them as holy and canonical but especially because the Holy Spirit witnesses in our hearts that they are from God . . ." (Article 5). Likewise the *Westminster Confession,* after noting the testimony of the church, "the heavenliness of the matter," and "many other incomparable excellencies" in the scriptures, concludes: "Yet, notwithstanding our full persuasion and assurance of the infallible truth and divine authority thereof, is from the inward work of the Holy Spirit, bearing witness by and with the Word in our hearts" (I,5).[8]

In addition to the profound theological insight found in this doctrine, there is also a practical lesson. Too often, we think we can prove the inspiration and authority of the scriptures by argumentation and impressive apologetics. A recent well-known illustration of this approach is seen in Harold Lindsell's *Battle for the Bible.*[9] Lindsell is concerned about establishing the trustworthiness of the Bible, but he rejects the classic Reformed approach and instead would have us place our confidence in inerrant "original autographs."[10] Lindsell has many critics[11] (and defenders), but one in particular faults him for failing to acknowledge the cruciality of the witness of the Spirit in this matter. That staunch Calvinist Lester De Koster, former editor of *The Banner*, maintains that "whenever we reject the Spirit's witness to the inspired Word (as does Lindsell), we are thrown back upon the shifting sands of human witness." He cites Calvin: "Let this point therefore stand: that those whom the Holy Spirit has inwardly taught, truly rest upon Scripture, and that Scripture indeed is self-authenticated; hence, it is not right to subject it to proof and reasoning" (I.7.5). Then De Koster declares, "The choice before us is clear. It is between Lindsell's rationalism and the 'inner testimony' affirmed by our Confession (Belgic). But it is a choice! Either rationalism *or* the Confession!"[12] To close this discussion with Calvin: "They who strive to build up firm faith in Scripture through disputation are doing things backwards" (I.7.4).

There are two other things which are more or less distinctive in the Reformed approach to scripture: a) the correlation of Word and Spirit and b) the covenant as a clue to scripture.

The Correlation of Word and Spirit. In addition to the idea of the internal witness of the Spirit, another distinctive of the Reformed tradition is the close correlation of Word and Spirit. Following Calvin, who in turn was greatly influenced by 2 Corinthians 3:6-8, Reformed confessions frequently link Word and Spirit. The Word without the Spirit can be a dead letter and produce a dead orthodoxy. The Spirit apart from the Word can lead into new doctrines and a one-sided experientialism which do not conform to God's objective revelation in his written Word.

The sentence in Calvin most frequently cited in this connection is found in I.9.3:

By a kind of mutual bond the Lord has joined together the certainty of his Word and of his Spirit so that the perfect (*solida*) religion of the Word may abide in our minds when the Spirit, who causes us to contemplate God's face, shines; and that we in turn may embrace the Spirit with no fear of being deceived when we recognize him in his own image, namely, in the Word.

This was originally directed against the Roman Catholics and the enthusiasts who, in different ways, separated Word and Spirit. But this exhortation is still relevant today. Moreover, as employed in the Reformed confessions, this correlation has relevance for almost every aspect of the life of the Christian. In the *Belgic Confession*, for example, it is related to faith. "We believe that this true faith, being wrought in man *by the hearing of the Word of God* and *by the operation of the Holy Spirit*, regenerates him and makes him a new man, causing him to live a new life, and freeing him from the bondage of sin" (Article 24, new Christian Reformed translation in *Psalter Hymnal* of 1976, emphasis mine; cf. *Heidelberg Catechism*, Q. 21).

Similarly, the church is also understood in terms of Word and Spirit. "I believe that from the beginning to the end of the world, and from among the whole human race, the Son of God, *by his Spirit and his Word*, gathers, protects, and preserves for himself, in the unity of the true faith, a congregation chosen for eternal life" (*Heidelberg Catechism*, Q. 54; cf. *Belgic Confession*, Article 27; *Canons of Dort* I,7; and *Westminster Confession* X,1).

Two more illustrations. In the *Belgic Confession* the sacraments are discussed in terms of Word and Spirit. God "has joined [the sacraments] to the Word of the Gospel the better to present to our senses both that which he gives us to understand *through his Word* and *that which he does inwardly in our hearts* (i.e., by the Holy Spirit), assuring and confirming in us the salvation which he imparts to us" (Article 33; cf. *Westminster Confession* XXVII,3). In the treatment of the second petition of the Lord's Prayer in the *Heidelberg Catechism*, the explanation of "Thy kingdom come" is most interesting. "That is, so govern us *by thy Word and Spirit* that we may more and more submit ourselves unto thee" (Q. 123).

The Covenant, the Clue to Scripture. If the Bible is to be the "infallible rule of faith and practice" (a phrase found in many Presbyterian and Reformed books of church order), the way the Bible is interpreted is crucial. One may have a very high view of the inspiration and authority of the Bible and then virtually ignore or distort much of its message. Without a proper hermeneutic (interpretive principle) the real message of the Bible may never be understood in its fullness or power. It is particularly important to understand the relation of the Old and New Testaments and the development of salvation history.

In the Reformed tradition, the covenant has provided this key. Zwingli stressed the significance of the covenant concept, and Calvin developed this notion further. In opposition to the Anabaptists of his day and other attempts ever since Marcion* to downgrade the Old Testament, Calvin maintained that there was fundamentally only one covenant, a covenant of grace.[13] The covenant takes on various forms in the development of redemptive history, but the substance of that covenant remains the same. Whether the covenant is made with Abraham, Moses, David, or Jeremiah, there is the same covenant promise: "I will be your God and you shall be my people." Moreoever, this promise has its substance and fulfillment in Jesus Christ (see II.9 and 10).

Calvin, like Luther, points to Christ as the focal point of scripture. "We must read Scripture," Calvin says, "expecting to find Christ there. Anyone who departs from this aim may labor and study all his life and never arrive at the knowledge of truth" (*Commentary on John*, 5:39; cf. *Commentary on Romans*, 10:4). However, focusing too narrowly on Christ as the sole meaning of scripture can lead to an unbiblical Christocentrism. By stressing the larger framework of the covenant, Reformed theology has a hermeneutical principle which does justice to the historical development and variety in God's revelation as well as the unity of revelation.[14]

---

*Marcion was a second-century heretic who believed that there was a total discontinuity between the Testaments.

Church Order

Most Reformed/Presbyterian Christians are aware of the fact that their system of church government is distinctive, but beyond that they are probably not aware of anything in their ecclesiology that makes them different. Peter Meinhold, however, a German specialist in various church traditions, states:[15]

> In its doctrine of the church the distinctiveness of the Reformed Church become particularly clear. Ecclesiology plays a much more prominent role in the Reformed confessions than in the Lutheran. This consists in the fact that Reformed ecclesiology includes church order and church discipline and frequently the doctrine of the word and sacraments as well.

Church order is often taken lightly by pastors as well as lay people, but when Calvin began his work in Geneva, one of his first concerns was to draw up a constitution (church order) for the church in Geneva.[16] (The other two things he considered essential for a well-ordered church were a confession of faith and a catechism.) This church order, as well as the later one of 1541, represented a compromise with the civil authorities in Geneva, but it expresses many of the features which still characterize Reformed and Presbyterian Churches today. (Recall, however, that not all churches in the Reformed tradition adhere to Presbyterian polity.)

Two things are crucial in Presbyterian church order. One is that the presbytery (classis) has taken the place of the bishop. Congregations select their own ministers and elect their elders and deacons, who together with the minister of the Word make up the consistory (session). But the consistory is amenable to the larger body. General Assemblies (or Synods), which are made up of approximately an equal number of lay and clergy delegates, can take certain actions, but major decisions affecting the government, worship, and beliefs of the denomination must be ratified by two-thirds (or three-fourths) of the presbyteries (classes). This represents a middle way between the "free" churches where each congregation is autonomous and the hierarchical churches where bishops have the ultimate authority.[17]

Of the three offices in Reformed/Presbyterian polity[18]—minister, elder, and deacon—the elder (or presbyter) is the key figure. Eugene Osterhaven maintains that this office "is of such importance to the polity of the Reformed Church that without it the church would lose its character as a Reformed Church.[19] The reason is that they are responsible for true preaching and the proper administration of the sacraments (the two classical Protestant marks or signs of the church). In short, they, together with the minister, are ultimately responsible for the spiritual well-being of the church.

The office of deacon is indispensable in another realm, that of finance, physical well-being, and benevolence—in short, service and compassion. This office has been neglected in some Presbyterian denominations,[20] but there is a growing appreciation for the wider possibilities of this office, especially as the church assumes greater responsibility in the realm of social righteousness and *diakonia*[21] (the Greek word for service or ministry). Thus the deacon's function, if properly understood, is a spiritual one which is related to the heart of the gospel (see IV.4.4). Where the lordship of Jesus Christ is properly stressed there will be no hierarchy, no lording it over one another in the body of Christ, but rather a servant ministry.[22]

L.J. Trinterud has succinctly and admirably summed up what is the nature of Calvin's—and true Presbyterian—church government:[23]

The primary elements of Calvin's theory of church government may be summed up in three. The church is a community or body in which Christ only is head, and all other members are equal under him. The ministry is given to the whole church, and is there distributed among many officers according as God has gifted and called them. All who hold office do so by election of the people whose representatives they are. The church is to be governed and directed by assemblies of officeholders, pastors, and elders, chosen to provide just representation for the church as a whole.

As Meinhold noted above, one of the distinctives of Reformed churchmanship is its understanding of discipline. In most Reformed church orders, it constitutes the third mark of the church. Calvin, like the Lutherans, only taught two marks of the church: the Word and the sacraments (IV.1.9). Why Calvin did not make discipline a mark of the church is not clear, for he was convinced that it was indispensable for a sound church.[24] "As the saving doctrine of Christ is the soul of the church, so does discipline serve as its own sinews, through which the members of the body hold together, each in its own place" (IV.12.1).[25] Not only that, those who do not practice discipline or who oppose it "are surely contributing to the ultimate dissolution of the church" (IV.12.1).

Therefore, when subsequent Reformed confessions made discipline the third mark of the church they were not deviating from the spirit of Calvin—or from the practice of Martin Bucer and John Knox who did consider discipline a third mark. Unfortunately, the true purpose of church discipline has not always been understood, and it has often been practiced in a harsh, unfeeling manner. Hence, the very word *discipline* evokes negative reactions from many people within Reformed Churches. However, its original and proper purpose in the Reformed Churches of Bucer, Calvin, and Knox was essentially positive, an aspect of pastoral care. It was an integral part of the proclamation of the Word of God whose goal was ultimately nothing other than the promoting of the holiness of the church and the honor of Christ.[26]

Church discipline, admittedly, is no longer practiced as it should be in many Reformed Churches, but it continues to be a characteristic concern of this tradition. Where properly administered, sinners are restored, heresy is refuted, the purity and unity of the church are safeguarded, and God is glorified.

Doctrine with a Purpose

It is commonly recognized that the Reformed tradition is theologically oriented. Presbyterian and Reformed believers, not to mention theologians, have always taken theology very seriously. In the classic words of the great German historian, Karl Holl, "The Calvinist knows *what* he believes and why he believes it."[27] A result has been a great concern for doctrinal clarity and purity. What may not be so well known is the classical Reformed concern for doctrine that is useful and profitable, and for truth that produces holiness. There is, in short, a practical, utilitarian bent in the Reformed fascination with theology, an active, ethical thrust of Reformed thought.

All this goes back to Calvin, who in turn was influenced by Bucer. Calvin hated "frigid speculation" and empty and vain philosophizing. Instead, he was constantly concerned with doctrine that was "sound and fruitful," "useful," and "profitable" (I.2.2; 5.9; 13.20).[28] He concedes, in his rather brief discussion of the Trinity, that those "who intemperately delight in speculation will not be satisfied." He justifies his brevity and straightforward approach on these grounds: "While I am zealous for the edification of the church, I felt I would be better advised not to touch upon many things that would profit but little and would burden my readers with useless trouble" (I.13.29).

Concern for truth, pure doctrine, and sound theology is important, but it should not be an end in itself. If this concern does not result in godliness and the edification of the church it has been perverted. If the approach of the *Heidelberg Catechism* is followed, there will be no problems here. This catechism, very much in the spirit of Calvin, after defining a doctrinal position, invariably asks what "advantage" or "benefit" comes from believing this truth (see Questions 28, 32, 36, 43, et al.). Note, moreoever, that already in Question 1 the *Catechism* "contains an ethics in embryo"[29] when it concludes that Jesus Christ "by his Holy Spirit makes me wholeheartedly willing and ready from now on to live for him."

This beautiful blending of belief and action, doctrine and ethics, finds classic expression in a phrase found in the "Form of Government" of *The Constitution of the Presbyterian Church, U.S.A.* (1928), Chapter I, Paragraph 4: "That truth is in order to goodness; and the great touchstone of truth, its tendency to promote holiness. . . . There is an inseparable connection between faith and practice, truth and duty. Otherwise, it would be of no consequence either to discover truth, or to embrace it."

The old cliche "not doctrine but life" is an untenable bifurcation still being promoted by die-hard liberals. The old liberal biblical scholar Morton Enslin can still write an essay entitled, "Religion without Theology," and conclude: "Thus it appears to me high time to declare a moratorium on theology and to stress as the real genius of our religion those values and virtues which result in a solid and wholesome manner of life and which enable men to achieve values which must result in a fuller, more useful, and so happier life."[30] Enslin's goal is a legitimate one; his error is in assuming that it can be obtained by ignoring theology. A cut-flower happiness or morality will soon wither away.

Two manifestations of this approach are seen in the Reformed accent on sanctification (in contrast to the Lutheran emphasis on justification), and the more general interest in ethics. Both these concerns stem from the so-called third use of the law. In contrast to Lutherans, who see the law largely in a negative light and stress its function in deepening our awareness of our sinfulness, in the Reformed tradition the "principal use" of the law is a positive one. That is, for the person already redeemed it serves as a stimulant and guide in living the Christian life (II.7.12-13).[31] This emphasis on the law, when perverted, produces a legalistic mentality. But properly understood, it produces a concern for obedience to the will of God in every sphere of life.

Moralism is avoided, however, by recognizing that a Reformed ethic is an ethic of gratitude. This is impressively illustrated in the structure of the *Heidelberg Catechism*. Only in Part III, which treats man's thankfulness and obedience (gratitude), do we find the exposition of the Ten Commandments and the Lord's Prayer. Ethical behavior is thus not so much a burden or obligation as an opportunity to express our gratitude to God for such a great salvation.[32]

A corollary of this ethic is a desire to do good works,[33] a stress on growth in the Christian life, and a quest for holiness (both personal and corporate). Whereas a favorite Lutheran phrase is *simul iustus et peccator* (justified and a sinner at the same time), the Reformed emphasis is on progress in the Christian life. "No man will be so unhappy," wrote Calvin, "but that he may every day make some progress, however small" (III.6.5). The same interest is found in the *Heidelberg Catechism* which constantly exhorts believers to "*more and more* die unto sin and live in a consecrated and blameless way" (Q. 70) and "*more and more* strengthen their faith and improve their life" (through partaking of the Lord's Supper, Q. 81). This "more and more" is also found in Questions 89, 115, and 123).[34]

Good works and the quest for holiness, however, must never be confused with a Pharisaical type of works-righteousness. Ethics and election are inseparable. This is the secret of the dynamic of Reformed activism. We are chosen in Christ "before the foundation of the world, that we should be holy and blameless before him" (Eph 1:4).[35]

A Life and World View

Calvinism can never be accused of having a God who is too small or a vision that is too narrow. From its powerful concept of a sovereign God whose will determines the destiny of men and nations to the vision of the glory of God which is manifest and acknowledged throughout the ends of the earth, Calvinism is a faith of the grand design. In contrast to Lutheranism's quest for a gracious God, pietism's concern for the welfare of the individual soul, and Wesleyanism's goal of personal holiness, the ultimate concern in the Reformed tradition transcends the individual and his salvation. It also goes beyond the church, the body of Christ. The concern is for the realization of the will of

God also in the wider realms of the state and culture, in nature and in the cosmos. In short, Reformed theology is kingdom theology.

This is attested in countless ways. First, there is Calvin's concern for civil government and the state, dramatically illustrated in the fact that in both the first and last editions of his great *Institutes* he concludes with a chapter on civil government. The catholicity of Calvin's concerns is generally recognized. In Geneva, he preached and taught, was a pastor and an administrator. But this was only the beginning of his involvement in the life of the city. He was also involved in economic, social, civil, and international affairs. The world was his parish; no aspect of life was alien to him.[36]

Calvin's mentor Martin Bucer, in addition to biblical commentaries and a variety of theological treatises, concluded his scholarly career by writing in 1550 his most significant work, *De Regno Christi* (On the Kingdom of Christ). It was written for the young English king Edward VI in the hope that, during his reign, the Reformation would not only be established in England but would also shape and penetrate the entire nation. His hope was that this work would provide the outlines for a Christian "discipline" which would order social as well as private life.[37] He addresses himself to questions of education, economics, social life, and politics in addition to the problems of the church. He thereby shows that he is closer to Calvin, and a Reformed ethos, than to Luther because he is convinced that "not only the church as an institution but the whole of human life, individual and social, must be ordered according to the will of God as revealed in the Bible."[38]

Further illustrations of this outlook are seen in the Puritans of the sixteenth and seventeenth centuries and the Dutch Calvinists of the late nineteenth and early twentieth centuries. The early English Puritans particularly emphasized personal regeneration and sanctification and a strict private and public morality. Later, however, in both Great Britain and North America they were to hold forth the vision of a holy commonwealth, a community in which every member should make the glory of God his sole concern.[39] Reverence for the Word of God and the idea of theocracy combined to foster

> the belief that New England was destined to be a "new Canaan," a land of godly people governed by a godly government, God being sovereign over all. This belief nourished an idealism which gave to New England Calvinism a liberating quality, a sense of predestined greatness, a vision of the coming of the glory of God amongst the people of the land.[40]

The Neo-Calvinists—Abraham Kuyper, Herman Bavinck, and their disciples—also sought in their own way to bring God's will to bear on the whole of Dutch society in a reform movement which began in the latter half of the nineteenth century. Although Bavinck was the greater theologian, it was Kuyper, the theologian-educator-prime minister, who was to have the greatest influence in this regard. In the Stone lectures, given at Princeton Seminary in 1898, he does not discuss traditional doctrines but rather considers Calvinism and politics, Calvinism and science, Calvinism and art, and Calvinism and the future. Only the second chapter deals with religion, as such, and here Kuyper's grand vision is expounded with passion.[41] A key question, he says, is whether religion is *partial*, i.e., limited only to the personal and private sectors of life, "or is it all-subduing and comprehensive—*universal* in the strict sense of the word?"[42] Then he develops his notion of "sphere-sovereignty,"[43] which has been so influential in the thinking of many Dutch Calvinists. It is now being promulgated in both North America and the Netherlands in a new form under the inspiration of the late philosopher of law in the Free University in Amsterdam, H. Dooyeweerd (and his colleague, D. Vollenhoven). Kuyper's outlook also is reflected in the thought of the influential Dutch theologian from Utrecht, the late A.A. van Ruler. Each of these men has his own distinctive position, and they in turn differ even more from the Puritans. What they have in common is a peculiarly Calvinistic approach to the world.

This conviction that the cause of Christ is not limited to individual believers or even the church finds eloquent expression in two modern Reformed confessions of faith, the *Foundations and Perspectives of Confession*[44] of the Netherlands Reformed Church and *Our Song of Hope,* a confessional statement in the Reformed Church in America. The former takes its point of departure in the proclamation of the kingdom of God, a major biblical theme which is rarely found in the confessions of the church. It begins with a section on "God, our King" and closes with this confidence: "When we consider the victory of Jesus Christ we do not despair of this earth, but remaining faithfully within it and aware of all that still resists God's reign, the Spirit constrains us to hasten patiently, to sigh joyfully, and wait actively for the complete revealing of God's glory over all his creation" (No. 18).

Our Song of Hope, in traditional Calvinistic fashion but in a fresh new way, notes that God's Spirit not only speaks through the scriptures and the church but also in the world "according to God's ultimate word in Christ," i.e., "in technology and business, in art and education God has not left himself without a witness" (Stanza 8). In Stanza 14, we read that "God's Spirit leads us into Truth," but not simply the truth of the salvation we have in Christ but also "into increasing knowledge of all existence." The last stanza (21), similar to the Dutch confession, ends with the kingdom theme even though the word is not used. "God will renew the world through Jesus. . . . There will be a new heaven and a new earth, and his creation will be filled with his glory."

A life and world view, a vision of the sovereignty of God and the lordship of Jesus Christ manifest in every sphere of life, a theology of the kingdom of God which transcends time and space—this is the grand design of Reformed theology at its best. Recent adherents—particularly Americans—have not always shared this vision, but it is certainly one of the chief characteristics of the classical Reformed tradition. As noted above, this vision takes many forms, but one leitmotif underlies them all: the glory of God.

A warning is also appropriate, especially in a tradition which is so alert to the dangers of idolatry. It comes from John Mackay, former president of Princeton Seminary and one of the past leaders of the World Alliance of Reformed Churches. In a lecture on "The Witness of the Reformed Churches Today," given over twenty-five years ago, he notes that, "in a very real sense, heritage determines destiny, and the road to tomorrow leads through yesterday." This is why it is important for members of any tradition to know their roots. But there is always the danger that the tradition, not the living God, will be glorified. Hence: "While we are unashamedly proud of our heritage, God grant that we may never take up toward it an idolatrous attitude, nor be bound and trammeled by it, for our fathers would not have wanted that to occur."[45]

"For from him and through him and to him are all things. To him be the glory forever! Amen" (Rom 11:36).

A Brief Annotated Bibliography

This bibliography is not exhaustive since it is not intended for specialists but primarily for laypersons and theological students. The bibliographies in the books cited will provide additional information for those who desire to investigate any particular topic more thoroughly.

I—Comprehensive Treatments of the Reformed Tradition

Bratt, John H., editor, *The Rise and Development of Calvinism: A Concise History* (Grand Rapids, Mich.: Wm. B. Eerdmans, 1959).

Bratt is Emeritus Professor of Bible at Calvin College in Grand Rapids. This work is similar to McNeill's (see below) but much shorter—and is out of print.

DeWitt, John R., *What Is the Reformed Faith?* (Carlisle, Pa.: The Banner of Truth Trust, 1981).

This came to my attention after completing the manuscript for this book. This book is a brief (24 pages) but very comprehensive, helpful analysis of "the great hall-marks of the Reformed Faith." Dr. DeWitt comes from the Reformed Church in America and is a Western Seminary graduate. He taught systematic theology for several years at the Reformed Seminary in Jackson, Mississippi, and is now a pastor of a Presbyterian Church in Memphis, Tennessee.

Leith, John, *An Introduction to the Reformed Tradition* (Richmond, Va.: John Knox Press, 1977).

Leith is a Southern Presbyterian historian/theologian and is a professor of theology at Union Seminary in Richmond, Virginia. This excellent exposition is similar to that of Osterhaven's (see below) but reflects more the Presbyterian milieu.

Mackay, John, *The Presbyterian Way of Life: What It Means to Live and Worship as a Presbyterian* (Englewood Cliffs, N.J.: Prentice-Hall, 1960).

Mackay is one of the best-known American Presbyterian leaders in the twentieth century. Former missionary, long-time president of Princeton Seminary, and a world-renowned ecumenical leader, he is basically writing about Reformed tradition and practice in this volume even though he uses the word "Presbyterian."

McNeill, John T., *The History and Character of Calvinism* (Oxford and New

113

York: Oxford University Press, 1967, and subsequent paperback editions).

The late John T. McNeill was one of America's foremost Calvin scholars. This work, unlike the two above, is largely historical and descriptive rather than theological.

Niesel, Wilhelm, *The Gospel and the Churches: A Comparison of Catholicism, Orthodoxy, and Protestantism* (Philadelphia: Westminster Press, 1962).

Niesel is one of the leading Calvin scholars in Germany and a former president of the World Reformed Alliance. The American title is a little misleading; the English title, *Reformed Symbolics,* is closer to the original. Niesel's approach is to take specific doctrines like the sovereignty of God or the doctrine of the church and compare the Lutheran and Reformed interpretations with those of the other major confessional groups.

Osterhaven, M. Eugene, *The Spirit of the Reformed Tradition* (Grand Rapids, Mich.: Wm. B. Eerdmans, 1971).

This outstanding portrayal of the Reformed tradition is now out of print, but some bookstores still have copies. Osterhaven is Professor of Systematic Theology at Western Seminary in Holland, Michigan.

Osterhaven, M. Eugene, *The Faith of the Church: A Reformed Perspective on Its Historical Development* (Grand Rapids, Mich.: Wm. B. Eerdmans, 1982).

This work is larger and more comprehensive than *The Spirit of the Reformed Tradition* (see above). Although written from a Reformed perspective, this study of the Christian faith is so irenic that it can be read with profit and appreciation by Christians of quite diverse backgrounds.

II—The Dutch Reformed Tradition

Kistemaker, Simon, *Calvinism: Its History, Principles and Perspectives* (Grand Rapids, Mich.: Baker Book House, 1966).

This small (104 pages) "study manual" contains a very brief biography of Calvin, a brief history of Calvinism, and then five chapters on some principles and perspectives of Calvinism. Kistemaker is of Christian Reformed background and professor of New Testament at the Reformed Theological Seminary in Jackson, Mississippi.

Kuyper, Abraham, *Lectures on Calvinism* (Grand Rapids, Mich.: Eerdmans, 1931/1953—still available as a paperback).

Kuyper and Herman Bavinck were two of the foremost Reformed theologians at the turn of the century. The six chapters of this book deal with topics such as politics, science, and art rather than with specific doctrines. They were originally given as the Stone Lectures at Princeton Seminary in 1898.

Plantinga, Cornelius, Jr., *A Place to Stand: A Reformed Study of Creeds and Confessions* (Grand Rapids, Mich.: Board of Publications of the Christian Reformed Church, 1979).

As far as I know, this is the first time the three Dutch American Reformed confessions—the *Heidelberg Catechism,* the *Belgic Confession,* and the *Canons of Dort*—have been treated in one book. The treatment of the ecumenical creeds—Apostles,' Nicene, and Athanasian—is very brief and serves largely as a preface to the full and very readable exposition of the three Reformed standards. This is designed for lay study groups and is a part of a set which contains a teacher's manual, posters, and the text of the Reformed standards.

Note: There are also smaller, separate treatments of the *Belgic Confession* by M.E. Osterhaven, and the *Canons of Dort* by G. Girod and H. Petersen.

III—The Heidelberg Catechism

The *Heidelberg Catechism* is *the* catechism not only of Reformed Churches of Dutch origin but also is the only standard of the German Reformed Church. It is also widely used in other countries such as Hungary, Switzerland, and Japan. Therefore, it merits separate treatment. The best commentaries in English (apart from a treatment by E.A. Dowey of Princeton Seminary which is not available in book form and the exposition by Plantinga cited above) are:

Barth, Karl, *The Heidelberg Catechism for Today* (Richmond, Va.: John Knox Press, 1964).

Barth, Karl, *Learning Jesus Christ Through the Heidelberg Catechism* (Grand Rapids, Mich.: Wm. B. Eerdmans, 1981).

Bruggink, Donald J., editor, *Guilt, Grace and Gratitude* (New York: Half Moon Press, 1963).

This symposium was commissioned by the Reformed Church in America to celebrate the four-hundredth anniversary of the catechism. The contributors are D. Bruggink, W. Burggraaff, J. Cook, J. De Jong, E. Eenigenburg, H. Hageman, E. Heideman, I.J. Hesselink, and E. Osterhaven.

Péry, André, *The Heidelberg Catechism with Commentary* (Philadelphia/ Boston: United Church Press, 1963).

This, too, is an anniversary edition and is fortunately still in print. This is generally more theological—and more Barthian—than the Reformed Church commentary, *Guilt, Grace and Gratitude,* but it is very readable. Péry is a French Swiss pastor in Geneva.

Thompson, Bard; Berkhof, Hendrikus; Schweizer, Eduard; and Hageman, Howard, *Essays on the Heidelberg Catechism* (Philadelphia/Boston: United Church Press, 1963).

This is a companion volume to the commentary by Péry. The first chapters deal with the historical background of the catechism; the other chapters treat key theological motifs and deal with questions like "Scripture and Tradition" and "The Catechism in Christian Nurture."

IV—*The Presbyterian (Scottish/American) Tradition*

Dowey, Edward A., Jr., *A Commentary on the Confession of 1967 and an Introduction to "The Book of Confessions"* (Philadelphia: Westminster Press, 1968).

This is intended first of all for United Presbyterians since over half of the book is on their new *Confession of 1967*. Part Two, however, contains a brief but helpful analysis of the other confessions adopted by the United Presbyterian Church in 1967 in addition to the *Westminster Confession* and *Shorter Catechism*. These include the *Scots Confession* of 1560 and the *Second Helvetic Confession*. Dowey is professor of the history of Christian doctrine at Princeton Theological Seminary.

Henderson, G.D., *Presbyterianism* (Aberdeen: The University Press, 1954).

This is largely a study of Presbyterian polity, not doctrines. The treatment is basically from a Scottish standpoint, but Henderson has also studied relevant literature about Reformed and Presbyterian Churches on the continent and in the U.S.A. The author is professor of church history, University of Aberdeen.

Hendry, George, *The Westminster Confession for Today: A Contemporary Interpretation* (Richmond, Va.: John Knox Press, 1960).

The title and subtitle indicate the nature of this study by the emeritus professor of theology at Princeton Theological Seminary.

Leith, John, *Assembly at Westminster: Reformed Theology in the Making* (Richmond, Va.: John Knox Press, 1973).

This study deals with both the background and the theology of the *Westminster Confession*. Since the scope is narrow, this work is more specialized than his later work cited earlier, *An Introduction to the Reformed Tradition*.

Rogers, Jack, *Scripture in the Westminster Confession* (Grand Rapids, Mich.: Wm. B. Eerdmans, 1976).

This thorough, penetrating study concentrates on only one aspect of the *Westminster Confession*; it illuminates many other subjects in this classic confession of Presbyterianism.

Skilton, John, editor, *Scripture and Confession: A Book About Confessions Old and New* (Philadelphia, Pa.: Presbyterian and Reformed Publishing Co., 1973).

This book is difficult to categorize since only one chapter is about the *Westminster Confession* (by John Murray). The authors are all from Westminster Seminary and are accordingly quite critical of the Presbyterian *Confession of 1967*. Thus this work and Dowey's—both valuable—

discuss some of the same questions from a rather different perspective; and both claim to represent true Presbyterianism!

Williamson, G.I., *The Westminster Confession of Faith: For Study Classes* (Philadelphia, Pa.: Presbyterian and Reformed Publishing Co., 1964).

This is a more popular, but very thorough, commentary on the *Westminster Confession.* The purpose is much the same as Plantinga's *A Place to Stand* (on the Dutch Reformed standards), i.e., to be a text for discussion groups. The author was an Orthodox Presbyterian home missionary in Massachusetts for several years before becoming a pastor of a Reformed congregation in New Zealand.

V—The German/Swiss Reformed Tradition

It is difficult to know which American books and authors to place in this category since 1) there has never been a Swiss Reformed Church in America and 2) the German Reformed Church in this country united in 1934 with the Evangelical Church (also of German background) to form the Evangelical and Reformed Church. This denomination, with the exception of a few congregations, united with the Congregational Church in 1957 to form the United Church of Christ.

The two theological seminaries which continue to reflect this older tradition to some extent are Lancaster Seminary in Pennsylvania and Eden Seminary in St. Louis.

To be complete, one should also add books by authors representing the Hungarian Reformed tradition in the United States. But there is only one theologian—Bela Vassady—who has produced any major works in English. He taught, for most of his career, at Lancaster Seminary.

Representatives of the German Reformed tradition cited elsewhere are Bard Thompson (under III) and Allen Miller (under VI,A). The leading American theologian whose roots are in this tradition is Donald Bloesch, Professor of Systematic Theology at Dubuque Theological Seminary (Presbyterian) in Iowa. His major work is *Essentials of Evangelical Theology,* two volumes (New York: Harper & Row, vol. 1, 1978; vol. 2, 1979).

Neibuhr, H. Richard, *Christ and Culture* (New York: Harper and Brothers, 1951).

H.R. Niebuhr, who taught most of his career at Yale Divinity School is less famous than his brother, Reinhold Niebuhr, who taught for many years at Union Theological Seminary in New York. Both came from and were ministers of the Evangelical and Reformed Church, but Richard was more Reformed in his orientation, Reinhold more Lutheran. Neither should be confused with Richard Reinhold Niebuhr (Richard's son) who teaches theology at Harvard Divinity School. In the above book Richard

Neibuhr opts for the Augustinian-Reformed position which he describes as "Christ the Transformer of Culture."

Schaff, Philip, *The Protestant Principle,* vol. 1 in the Lancaster series on Mercersburg Theology, edited by Bard Thompson and George Bricker (Philadelphia/Boston: United Church Press, 1964. Originally appeared in English in 1845).

Schaff, Swiss-born and German-trained, was the most famous German Reformed historian/theologian in the United States in the late nineteenth century. He began his career in the United States at the German Reformed Seminary in Mercersburg, Pennsylvania. He then taught from 1870 until his death in 1893 at Union Seminary in New York. He is best known for his *History of the Christian Church* (8 vols.).

Schroeder, Frederick, *Worship in the Reformed Tradition* (Philadelphia/Boston: United Church Press, 1966).

Schroeder, who is also the author of *Preaching the Word with Authority* (1954) is president emeritus of Eden Theological Seminary in Eden Groves, Missouri. For many years he was a pastor in the Evangelical and Reformed Church.

Vassady, Bela, *The Main Traits of Calvin's Theology* (Grand Rapids, Mich.: Eerdmans, 1951).

—*Christ's Church: Evangelical, Catholic and Reformed* (Grand Rapids, Mich.: Eerdmans, 1965).

Vassady is of Hungarian Reformed background. His major work is a small, one-volume systematic theology entitled *Light Against Darkness* (Philadelphia: The Christian Education Press, 1961).

VI—Some Source Books

What makes the Reformed tradition different from Lutheran, Anglican, or Methodist is the variety of church "fathers" and the multiplicity of confessions and catechisms. Those who wish to explore the Reformed tradition in depth should consult and compare confessions other than those of their own particular tradition. Unfortunately, no single book (in English) contains them all.

A. The Standards of the Reformed (RCA) and Christian Reformed (CRC) Churches

The *Heidelberg Catechism,* translated by Allen Miller and M. Eugene Osterhaven (Boston/Philadelphia: United Church Press, 1962).

This new translation was commissioned for the 1963 anniversary year by the North American Alliance of Reformed and Presbyterian Churches. It is not only an excellent translation but also has the advantage of being available in a small, convenient (and reasonable) format. The CRC version of the *Heidelberg Catechism* is also available separately.

Liturgy and Psalms, Gerrit T. Vander Lugt, editor (New York: The Board of Education, 1968).

This volume should be in the home of every RCA member. It contains not only all of the orders for worship, the *Psalter,* a treasury of prayers, but also the *Heidelberg Catechism* (Miller-Osterhaven translation), the *Belgic Confession,* and the *Canons of Dort* (both translated by Vander Lugt).

Ecumenical Creeds and Reformed Confessions (Grand Rapids, Mich.: Board of Publications of the Christian Reformed Church, 1979).

This is the Christian Reformed version of the three standards, all in fresh translation. Particularly noteworthy is the fine verse style of the translation of the catechism. This volume also has the advantage of being handier and cheaper than the RCA *Liturgy and Psalms.*

B. More General Collections

Cochrane, Arthur, *Reformed Confessions of the Sixteenth Century* (Philadelphia, Pa.: Westminster Press, 1966).

This is the first collection of Reformed sixteenth-century confessions in English. The only problem is that certain key confessions such as the *Canons of Dort* and the *Westminster Confession,* which were produced in the seventeenth century, are not included.

Gerrish, Brian, *The Faith of Christendom: A Sourcebook of Creeds and Confessions* (Cleveland and New York: The World Publishing Co., Meridian Books, 1963).

As an illustration of Reformed confessions Gerrish chooses the *Gallican* (or French) *Confession of 1559.* It reflects the theology and spirit of Calvin and was a major influence on the *Belgic Confession.* The long introduction is superb. This volume is similar to Leith's, noted below, but is not as complete.

Leith, John H., *Creeds of the Churches: A Reader in Christian Doctrine from the Bible to the Present. Revised Edition* (Richmond, Va.: John Knox Press, 1973).

There are only three Reformed confessions in this large (597 pages) collection: The *Ten Conclusions of Berne* (1528); the *Second Helvetic Confession* (1566); and the *Westminster Confession* (1646). The introductions are most helpful.

Schaff, Philip, *The Creeds of Christendom: With a History and Critical Notes,* three volumes (New York, 1877; sixth edition 1931, and subsequent reprintings, the latest being by Baker Book House in 1977).

Some of the introductions are dated and inadequate, and we now have many of these creeds/confessions in newer translations, but "nothing yet has appeared in the English-speaking world to challenge Schaff's suprem-acy. Even on the continent of Europe there is no comparable work" (B. Gerrish). Schaff, a German-American Reformed scholar, was the leading church historian of his day.

Thompson, Bard, *Liturgies of the Western Church* (Cleveland and New York: World Publishing Co.-Meridian Books, 1962).

Since faith, worship, and theology are inextricably intertwined, it is important to include this collection as well. Here one can compare the earliest Reformed liturgies of Zwingli (1525) and Bucer (1539) with those of Calvin (1545), Knox (1556), and *The Westminster Directory* (1644).

Torrance, T.F., *The School of Faith: The Catechisms of the Reformed Church* (New York: Harper, 1959).

Catechisms are often not included in books of creeds and confessions; hence this volume is especially valuable (but, alas! out of print). Torrance, Scotland's leading theologian, here gathers all the Reformed catechisms which have been used since the Reformation in the Church of Scotland, including Calvin's *Geneva Catechism* of 1541 and some (such as *Craig's Catechism*) not known in the U.S.A. In addition, Torrance contributes a 126-page introduction on the theology of these catechisms.

Concluding Note

Those who are really interested in the Reformed tradition should go back to its most formative influence and chief source, John Calvin himself. Other Reformed leaders are important—Zwingli, Bucer, Bullinger, and Knox, to name only a few. But *the* theologian of the Reformation is Calvin, and his *Institutes of the Christian Religion* is an enduring classic, a book that has changed the world. Even today, Calvin is more readable and relevant than most modern theology. The best translation is by Ford Lewis Battles in the Library of Christian Classics edition, edited by John T. McNeill (Phila-delphia, Pa.: Westminster Press, 1960, and frequent reprintings).

Laypersons who do not want to invest in the large two-volume set of the *Institutes* but who would like to savor something of Calvin's writings should purchase *John Calvin: Selections from His Writings*, edited by John Dillen-berger (originally published in 1971, a Doubleday Anchor Original, now available from The Scholars' Press in Missoula, Montana—for a much higher price).

This large paperback (590 pages) contains a brief introduction to Calvin's life and work, some of his letters, including the famous *Reply to Cardinal Sadolet,* the ecclesiastical ordinances for the Church of Geneva, selections from his *1545 Catechism* and the *Institutes,* and several treatises, including the beautiful short treatise on the Lord's Supper.

All in all, a wonderful collection with helpful introductions by a competent Reformation scholar.

Notes

Preface

1. *The Reformed Review* 27, no. 2 (Winter 1974), pp. 103ff.

Introduction

1. Wilhelm Niesel, *Was heisst reformiert?* (Munich: Kaiser Verlag, 1934).
2. E.g., Traditional (i.e., nineteenth-century) Dutch Calvinism; Pietistic; Ecumenical; Contemporary Dutch (especially Van Ruler); Old Princeton School (especially Charles Hodge); Nineteenth-Century German Reformed, including the Mercersburg Theology; "High" Reformed; Social-Integrationists; etc. There are also crypto-Arminians, crypto-liberals, and not so crypto-fundamentalists among us. The last are only "Reformed" in name and belong to the RCA (or Christian Reformed, or various Presbyterian denominations, or the United Church of Christ) because of tradition or convenience.
3. James I. McCord, "A Frank Evaluation of the State of the Church," *The Presbyterian Layman* (January 1977), p. 8.

Chapter One

1. See M. Eugene Osterhaven, *The Spirit of the Reformed Tradition* (Grand Rapids, Mich.: Eerdmans, 1971), pp. 171-76.
2. Strong's *Systematic Theology* first came out in 1907 and was still one of the recommended texts when I came to Western Seminary in 1951.
3. His last years were spent as a visiting professor at Calvin College and Seminary. There he and his wife joined a local Christian Reformed congregation shortly before his death on November 22, 1979.
4. The origins of this famous slogan are obscure. It does not come from Calvin but a later period. See the thorough study of the Hungarian-Swiss scholar Gyula Barczay, *Ecclesia semper reformanda* (Zurich: EVZ-Verlag, 1961).

Chapter Two

1. Some of the denominations which are allegedly non-confessional, such as Baptists and Congregationalists, nevertheless sometimes have statements

of faith which, for all practical purposes, are nearly the same as creeds.

2. J.K.S. Reid, ed., *Calvin: Theological Treatises* (Philadelphia: Westminster, 1965), p. 26. This confession is also found in *Reformed Confessions of the Sixteenth Century*, ed. Arthur Cochrane (Philadelphia: Westminster, 1966), p. 120.

3. "In the Reformed Confessions the question of the arrangement of the doctrine of the Word of God, like that of election, is particularly stressed" (Paul Jacobs, *Theologie Reformierter bekenntnisschriften in Grundzugen* [Neukirchen Kreis Moers: Neukirchener Verlag, 1959], p. 105, tr. mine).

4. See my article, "Reformed, but Ever Reforming," *Church Herald*, October 18, 1974, pp. 6-7, and Cornelius Van Til's response in *The Banner*, November 7, 1975 ("Letter to the Editor"). Cf. Osterhaven, *Spirit of the Reformed Tradition*, pp. 34-35; and George S. Hendry, "Gospel, Confession and Scripture," in *A Reexamination of Lutheran and Reformed Traditions*, ed. W.A. Quanbeck and G.S. Hendry (published jointly by the North America Area of the World Alliance of Reformed Churches and the U.S.A. National Committee of the Lutheran World Federation, 1964).

5. Exceptions might be the Orthodox Presbyterian (OPC) and Presbyterian Church in America (PCA), which maintain a rather rigid adherence to the *Westminster Confession*.

6. Karl Barth, *The Word of God and the Word of Man* (original title: *Das Wort Gottes und die Theologie* [1924]; first published in the United States by Zondervan in 1935; subsequently published as a Harper Torchbook from 1957), pp. 234-35 (in 2nd. edition).

7. Cochrane, *Reformed Confessions*, p. 15.

8. "If we could have in the twentieth century credal discussion as vigorous as that which characterized the fourth century, it would be a very healthy phenomenon. . . . The sooner it starts the better." So says Paul Woolley, former professor of Church History at Westminster Theological Seminary, in "What Is a Creed For? Some Answers from History," in *Scripture and Confession*, ed. John H. Skilton (Philadelphia: Presbyterian and Reformed Publishing Co., 1973), p. 124.

9. E.P. Heideman provides an illuminating analysis of the relation of the Dutch Reformed Church to her written confessions on the basis of Article X, Section One, of its new church order of 1950 in an essay, "The Confession of the Fathers," *Reformed Review* 9 (January 1956), pp. 34-41.

10. *Minutes of General Synod, RCA* (172nd Regular Session, June 12-16, 1978, p. 37. The background for this confession is found on pp. 35f. Note that a draft was approved in 1974 as a provisional confession for use in the churches.

11. *Our Song of Hope* is published by Wm. B. Eerdmans Publishing Co. (1975) together with a commentary on the text, also by Heideman.

12. On the RCA and its approach to confessions, see Isaac C. Rottenberg,

"The Confessional Life of the Church," *Reformed Review* 15 (March 1962), pp. 28-36.

13. See Norman Shepherd, "Scripture and Confession," in Skilton, *Scripture and Confession,* pp. 3ff.

14. M.E. Osterhaven, *Our Confession of Faith* (Grand Rapids, Mich.: Baker Book House, 1964), p. 12.

15. "Nobody is able to read the Scriptures without choosing a center in the light of which he reads all other parts of the Bible" (Eduard Schweizer, "Scripture and Tradition: The Problem," in *Essays on the Heidelberg Catechism,* by Bard Thompson et al. [Philadelphia/Boston: United Church Press, 1963], p. 131).

16. Skilton, *Scripture and Confession,* p. 122.

Chapter Three

1. John Leith even declares, "The Reformed tradition has always hesitated to declare itself fully in regard to the office of deacon, and for this reason the office of deacon cannot be made a principle of Presbyterianism," (*Introduction to the Reformed Tradition* [Atlanta: John Knox Press, 1977], p. 156). But then he concedes that the office merits serious attention, especially as depicted by Reformed scholars such as Eugene Heideman in his *Reformed Bishops and Catholic Elders* (Grand Rapids, Mich.: Eerdmans, 1970), pp. 124f.

2. A new, original rationale for the fourth office has been provided by the Theological Commission of the Reformed Church in America. See *Minutes of General Synod RCA* (174th Regular Session, June 16-20, 1980, pp. 111ff.). *The* study of this subject is by Robert W. Henderson, *The Teaching Office in the Reformed Tradition* (Philadelphia: Westminster Press, 1962).

3. "The importance of church order can hardly be overemphasized, and Reformed churches recognize that fact. Moreover, the government of the church in its broad detail is a part of its doctrine" (Osterhaven, *Spirit of the Reformed Tradition,* p. 61).

4. John Calvin, *Institutes of the Christian Religion,* ed. John T. McNeill (Philadelphia: Westminster, 1960), IV.10.30. He concludes this section with this gentle admonition: "Love will best judge what may hurt or edify; if we let love be our guide, all will be safe."

5. Leith, *Introduction,* pp. 138-39.

6. This is affirmed beautifully in the *First Helvetic Confession* (1536): "Christ himself is the only true and proper head and shepherd of his church. He gives to his church shepherds and teachers who at his command administer the Word and office of the keys in an orderly and regular fashion . . ." (Article 18).

7. Emile Doumergue, *Jean Calvin: Les Hommes et les choses de son temps* 5 (Lausanne: Georges Bridel, 1910), p. 6.

8. Osterhaven, *Spirit*, p. 65. See also the fine treatments of G.D. Henderson, *Presbyterianism* (Aberdeen: The University Press, 1954), chapter IV, "Origins of the Eldership"; and Heideman, *Reformed Bishops*, chapter 6, "Who Is an Elder?"

9. See Francois Wendel, *Calvin* (New York: Harper & Row, 1963), pp. 72-93, 77-78, 304-5; and Henderson, pp. 66ff.

10. Leith, *Introduction*, pp. 157-58. See also G.D. Henderson, pp. 47f.

11. Originally, that is, in the sixteenth century, Puritanism was a movement within the Church of England (Anglican) to promote reform along Calvinistic lines. Later, when they were forced out of the established church, they became Presbyterians, Congregationalists, and Baptists. They stressed personal regeneration, sanctification, sabbatarianism, and a strict morality. Thus they represented a type of Calvinism, but went beyond Calvin and modified his views in some important ways. See Peter Toon, *Puritans and Calvinism* (Swengel, Pa.: Reiner Publications, 1973).

12. Wilhelm Niesel, "Our Witness in the Ecumenical Movement Today," in the *Reformed and Presbyterian World* (December 1965). See also Heideman, *Reformed Bishops*, esp. pp. 38f., 159f.

13. Henderson, *Presbyterianism*, p. 174.

Chapter Four

1. This definition is found in the Introduction to the first American edition of the *Constitution of 1793* of the Reformed Church in America. See Chapter 1 in *A Companion to the Liturgy: A Guide to Worship in the Reformed Church in America,* ed. Garrett C. Roorda (New York: The Half Moon Press, 1971).

2. All of these liturgies can be found in Bard Thompson, *Liturgies of the Western Church* (Cleveland and New York: World Publishing Co.-Meridian Books, 1962).

3. See Howard Hageman's earlier book on Reformed liturgies, *Pulpit and Table* (Richmond, Va.: John Knox Press, 1962).

4. Howard G. Hageman, "The Liturgical Revival," *Theology Today* (January 1950), pp. 490ff.

5. A revision of the 1968 *Liturgy* is now in process by the Worship Commission of the RCA.

6. *Liturgy,* p. 65.

7. Ibid.

8. Ibid., p. 79. This is from the earlier order in the *Liturgy and Psalms* of 1906.

9. (Cochrane, *Reformed Confessions,* p. 286). Similarly, in the *Belgic Confession,* "The manner in which we partake of them [Christ's body and blood] is not by the mouth but by the Spirit through faith" (Article 35).

10. Recent Zwingli scholars maintain that Zwingli had a higher view of the sacrament than is traditionally attributed to him. See Jacques Courvoisier, *Zwingli, A Reformed Theologian* (Richmond: John Knox Press, 1963), pp. 67-77. See also Wilhelm Niesel, *Gemeinschaft mit Jesus Christus* (C. Kaiser, 1964), pp. 136ff.

11. John Calvin, *Institutes of the Christian Religion,* ed. John T. McNeill (Philadelphia: Westminster Press, 1960).

12. In that era Roman Catholic laity were permitted to partake of the Mass only once a year! See also p. 1421, note 39, in McNeill, *Institutes.*

13. See the section, "Calvin the Preacher," in T.H.L. Parker, *John Calvin: A Biography* (Philadelphia: Westminster Press, 1961), pp. 89-96. See also Parker's older work, the best in English on Calvin's preaching, *The Oracles of God: An Introduction to the Preaching of Calvin* (London: Lutterworth Press, 1947).

14. It is strange that this high view of preaching has been virtually ignored by subsequent Reformed/Presbyterian theologians except for Karl Barth. In his *Church Dogmatics* I, he has a chapter on "The Word of God in Its Threefold Forms," the first of which is "The Word of God as Preached" (Edinburgh: T.&T. Clark, 1932), pp. 98ff.

15. See J.J. von Allmen, *Preaching and Congregation* (Richmond, Va.: John Knox Press, 1962), chapter 5, "Preaching as the Reformed Church's Contribution to the Ecumenical Movement."

16. A new Reformed Church hymnal, *Rejoice in the Lord,* ed. the late Eric Routley, is scheduled for publication in June 1984.

17. See their *Trinity Hymnal,* published in 1961 by the Orthodox Presbyterian Church.

18. See their *Psalter Hymnal,* published in 1976 by the Christian Reformed Church Board of Publications.

19. Barth, *Church Dogmatics* I, 2, p. 257.

20. Some examples of interdenominational hymnals which do not measure up to Reformed standards of worship (and theology): *Living Praise Hymnal,* compiled by John W. Peterson (1974); *Favorite Hymns of Praise* (Tabernacle Publishing Company, 1974); *The New Church Hymnal,* ed. Ralph Carmichael (1976); *Praise!* (Zondervan, 1979); *Living Hymns* (Encore Publications, 1979); *Hymns for the Family of God,* ed. Fred Bock (with considerable influence of William and Gloria Gaither, 1965). This hymnal, however, is superior to those listed above.

21. Published by Hope Publishing Co.

22. Cited in Hageman, *Pulpit and Table,* p. 15. A recent editorial by RLW in the Lutheran theological quarterly, *Dialog* 17 (Winter 1978), p. 4, makes a similar point:

> We experience the presence of God in the liturgy, and even as we bring more sophisticated and critical thinking to our faith, the liturgy

continues to touch us at a deep, almost primal, level of our life. . . . Indeed, the liturgy . . . is composed largely of material drawn directly from the Scriptures, and the way we interpret the Scriptures is formed as much by the liturgy as by any other activity in our life.

23. From the foreword to Hageman, *Pulpit and Table,* p. 7.

Chapter Five

1. The word *scholasticism* comes from the Latin word *schola* from which we get the words *scholar* and *scholarly.* So far so good. But when scholars or their scholarship become divorced from life and the so-called "real world," we start getting the negative connotations of *scholasticism.*

   Similarly, the word *rationalistic* comes from the Latin word *ratio,* which means reason. To be reasonable or rational is desirable, but when reason is separated from faith and experience and opposed to revelation, it becomes a questionable guide.

2. Philip Schaff, *The Principle of Protestantism* (first edition 1844; new edition published as the first volume of the Lancaster series on Mercersburg Theology. Philadelphia/Boston: United Church Press, 1964, p. 130.)

   A similar, and equally trenchant, criticism is made by the great Scottish theologian, T.F. Torrance, emeritus professor of dogmatics at the University of Edinburgh: The "immediate reason" for the "wilderness of irrationality and confusion" in the church today, he suggests, "is the deep cleavage that has opened up between theology and experience. Detached from the empirical reality of the living and acting God, theology tended to become abstract and rationalistic and got stuck in arid ideas and inflexible frames of thought, losing its relevance for the life of faith" (*God and Rationality* [London/New York: Oxford University Press, 1971], p. 3).

3. Aquinas was not the first theologian, however, to utilize Aristotle's philosophy. As early as the sixth century, Boethius used Aristotelian logic for explaining the creeds. A major difference is that Aquinas was also greatly influenced by the Arabian commentators on Aristotle, viz., Avicenna (980-1037) and Averroes (1126-1198).

4. See Bengt Hagglund, *History of Theology,* third edition (St. Louis: Concordia, 1966), chapters 17-19. Hagglund distinguishes between "older," "high," and "late" scholasticism.

5. Calvin rarely refers to Aquinas in his writings, but often to Lombard and always in a disparaging way. Lombard's *Four Books of Sentences* was the most widely used theological textbook from 1215 on, until it was eventually replaced by Aquinas' *Summa.*

6. See the outline of Beza's discussion of the decrees of God in Heinrich Heppe, *Reformed Dogmatics,* revised and ed. Ernst Bizer (London: Allen and Unwin, 1950), pp. 147-48. This work first appeared in 1861.

7. Generous selections from all three of these theologians are found in a more recent volume entitled *Reformed Dogmatics,* ed. John W. Beardslee III, in "A Library of Protestant Thought" (New York: Oxford University Press, 1965; reprinted in a paperback edition by Baker Book House).

8. One of the differences between Emil Brunner and Karl Barth is that the former scorned this approach, whereas the latter was very appreciative (though not uncritical) of it. Barth interacted with these theologians constantly in his *Church Dogmatics.* In his foreword to Heppe's *Reformed Dogmatics* (London: George Allen & Unwin, Ltd., 1950) he notes that these late sixteenth- and seventeenth-century Reformed, "orthodox" theologians were very different from the nineteenth-century liberalism with which he had become disillusioned. They were concerned not simply about the "much appealed-to life" (of liberalism) but also about *truth* in a very serious way. He was astonished "at its wealth of problems and the sheer beauty of its trains of thought" (p. vi).

9. These pairings are only suggestive and are by no means exhaustive. For example, both Luther and Calvin were influenced by the Augustianian revival of the Renaissance period, and Tillich was influenced by Hegel as much as or more than Barth.

10. Cited in G.D. Henderson, *Presbyterianism,* p. 23.

11. Berkhof's *Manual of Reformed Doctrine* (1933) has been used for many years by older Reformed Church ministers in the Midwest to examine candidates for the ministry. Until about twenty years ago, his *Systematic Theology* (1938) was still used as a text at Presbyterian Seminaries like Princeton and Austin. Note that L. Berkhof, who taught at Calvin Seminary from 1906 to 1944 (d. 1957) is in no way related to the Dutch theologian, Hendrikus Berkhof (author of *Christ the Meaning of History, Doctrine of the Holy Spirit,* and *Christian Faith*), who is an emeritus professor at the University of Leiden.

12. Scottish Realism and a related school of thought, Scottish Common Sense Philosophy, flourished in Scotland in the late eighteenth and early nineteenth centuries. Both stressed that man's knowledge is dependent not on experience or inductive reasoning but on general rational principles which we know by intuition and which are self-evident and universally valid. This philosophy had impact on one of American Presbyterianism's most influential theologians, Archibald Alexander, who taught at Princeton Seminary from 1811 to 1851. See the essay by John C. Vander Stelt, "Archibald Alexander: Inconsistent Empiricism and Theory of Scripture," in *Hearing and Doing: Philosophical Essays Dedicated to H. Evan Runner,* ed. John Kraay and Anthony Tol (Toronto: Wedge Publishing Foundation, 1979), pp. 159ff.

13. H. Evan Runner, *The Relation of the Bible to Learning* (Rexdale, Ontario: The Association for Reformed Scientific Studies, 1967), pp. 81-83.

14. See Jack B. Rogers and Donald K. McKim, *The Authority and Interpre-*

tation of the Bible (San Francisco and New York: Harper and Row, 1979), pp. 185ff., "A Summary of the Shifts that Produced Reformed Scholasticism"; and pp. 289ff., "The Influence of Scottish Realism." They also show on pp. 330ff. how this philosophy influenced another staunch Presbyterian theologian, B.B. Warfield (1851-1921).

15. Cited in Rogers and McKim, *Authority,* p. 197, n. 247.

16. Carl Henry, *God, Revelation and Authority* (Waco, Texas: Word Books), vols. 1 and 2 appeared in 1976, vols. 3 and 4 in 1979, vol. 5, part one in 1982.

17. Kenneth Briggs in the *New York Times.* Richard Ostling, religion editor of *Time* magazine, also claims that this work "establishes Henry as the leading theologian of the nation's growing evangelical flank" (both quotations taken from the dust jacket). I would contend that Professor Donald Bloesch of Dubuque Seminary can lay better claim to that distinction. See his *Essentials of Evangelical Theology* (San Francisco and New York: Harper and Row, vol. 1, 1978, vol. 2, 1979), plus thirteen other volumes written during the last fifteen years, during which time Carl Henry produced no major works.

18. Henry, *God,* vol. 1, p. 229.

19. Ibid., vol. 3, pp. 389 and 476.

20. Bloesch, *Essentials,* vol. 2, p. 267.

21. Ibid., p. 268.

22. McNeill, ed., *Institutes,* p. 11.

23. See the late Ford Lewis Battles' beautiful book, *The Piety of John Calvin: An Anthology Illustrative of the Spirituality of the Reformer* (Grand Rapids, Mich.: Baker Book House, 1978). See also a recent work with a similar title but quite different approach by the Roman Catholic theologian, Lucien Joseph Richard, *The Spirituality of John Calvin* (Richmond, Va.: John Knox Press, 1974).

24. See Hesselink, "The Development and Purpose of Calvin's *Institutes,*" *Reformed Review* 23 (Spring 1970).

25. Jean-Daniel Benoit, *Calvin Directeur d'Ames* (Strasbourg: Editions Oberlin, 1947), p. 14. (Translation mine.)

26. See T.F. Torrance, *The School of Faith* (London: James Clarke, 1959), pp. xviff.: "The Contrast between the Reformation and the Westminster Catechisms."

27. I am thinking particularly of his popular digest of his four-volume *Reformed Dogmatics* (of which only one volume is available in English), unfortunately entitled in English, *Our Reasonable Faith* (Eerdmans, 1956). The original title is *Magnalia Dei,* i.e., "The Wonderful Works of God."

28. See especially his impressive fourteen-volume series, *Studies in Dogmatics,* published by Eerdmans. The first volume to appear in English was *The Providence of God* (1952), the last *The Church* (1976). Berkouwer's work is impressive not only for his tremendous erudition but also the doxological

character of his theology. That is, when confronted by inexplicable mysteries of the faith he will conclude with an outburst of praise to God.

29. See above, note 8, for a list of some of his publications in English. His major work is a one-volume systematic theology, *Christian Faith: An Introduction to the Study of the Faith* (Grand Rapids, Mich.: Eerdmans, 1979). He says in the preface that he wants the book "to be both informative and inspirational" (p. xi). That is a rare goal for a systematic or dogmatic theology!

30. T.F. Torrance, *A Calvin Treasury*, ed. W.F. Keesecker (London: SCM Press, 1968), p. viii. Torrance, because of his affinity with Karl Barth, would be considered by Henry Van Til et al. as an irrationalist. Ironically, he has written *God and Rationality* (London and New York: Oxford University Press, 1969). Torrance is a staunch defender of the rational, scientific character of theology but, at the same time, is quite opposed to the scholastic approach.

31. Mackay, *The Presbyterian Way of Life* (Englewood Cliffs, N.J.: Prentice-Hall, 1960), pp. 9-10. See also George Brown, "Piety and the Reformed Tradition," *Reformed Review* 23, Spring 1970, pp. 143ff.

Chapter Six

1. Election and predestination are often equivalent terms for the divine choice of persons to salvation (see the use of both terms in the definition from the *Second Helvetic Confession* cited below). *Election*, however, is often a broader term referring to the election of Israel or the church, whereas *predestination* refers more to the predetermination by God of the individual's ultimate destiny. *Providence* is the doctrine that God preserves and governs his whole creation by his power and according to his will.

2. Paul Jacobs, *Prädestination und Verantwortlichkeit* (Predestination and Responsibility). This appeared originally in 1937, but was reprinted in 1968 by the Wissenschaftliche Buchgesellschaft in Darmstadt, Germany.

3. See Harry Buis, *Historic Protestantism and Predestination* (Philadelphia: Presbyterian and Reformed Publishing Co., 1958).

4. Martin Luther, *The Bondage of the Will*, trans. J.L. Packer and O.R. Johnston (London: James Clarke, 1957), p. 169.

5. For documentation see Wilhelm Niesel, *The Gospel and the Churches: A Comparison of Catholicism, Orthodoxy, and Protestantism* (Philadelphia: Westminster Press, 1962. The British title of this work is *Reformed Symbolics*), pp. 234ff.

6. This emphasis comes to the fore in two key confessional statements of the seventeenth century: *The Canons of Dort* (1618-1619) and *The Westminster Confession* (1646). In the latter, for example, we read (Chapter III, Section VII):

The rest of mankind [the non-elect] God was pleased, according to the unsearchable counsel of his own will, whereby he extendeth or withholdeth mercy as he pleaseth, for the glory of his sovereign power over his creatures, to pass by, and to ordain them to dishonor and wrath for their sin, to the praise of his glorious justice. (In *Creeds of the Churches,* ed. John Leith [Garden City, N.Y.: Anchor Books, 1963], p. 199.)

Cf. similar statements in the *Canons of Dort,* Articles 6 and 15.

7. Cochrane, *Reformed Confessions,* p. 240. Note the prominence of the place of Christ in predestination. Later in this chapter in the *Second Helvetic Confession* Bullinger repeats Calvin's famous phrase, "Christ is the mirror in whom we may contemplate our predestination" (p. 242). See below, note 10.

8. *The Instruction in Faith* was written in French and appeared in 1537, the year after the first edition of Calvin's *Institutes.* The following year, Calvin produced a Latin version of his first catechism. This was translated and published privately by Ford Lewis Battles in 1972. These catechisms form an important link between the first (1536) and the second (1539) editions of the *Institutes* and are not to be confused with Calvin's later, better-known so-called *Genevan Catechism* of 1545.

9. "No other sentence [Eph 1:3-4] that Paul wrote carries more mystery into our union with Christ than this doxology. And the doxology can be spoiled by trading the mystery for a crisp formula," Lewis B. Smedes, *All Things Made New: A Theology of Man's Union with Christ* (Grand Rapids, Mich.: Eerdmans, 1970), p. 117. Smedes gives an excellent exposition of this key text.

10. *Institutes* III.24.5. Emphasis mine. Calvin says virtually the same thing in a polemical tract, his *Refutation of Pighius* in *Concerning the Eternal Predestination of God,* trans. and ed. by J.K.S. Reid (London: James Clarke, 1961), p. 127: "Christ therefore is for us the bright mirror of the eternal and hidden election of God, and also the earnest and the pledge."

11. Cf. their respective commentaries on Romans 9:14f., Dodd in the Moffatt series, Hunter in the Torch series. A modern theologian who has wrestled seriously—and creatively—with these passages is Karl Barth. See his *Church Dogmatics* II, 2, (Edinburgh: T.&T. Clark,) chapter 7, especially pp. 306ff. Barth interprets both election and reprobation in such a radically Christocentric way that reprobation (i.e., damnation) is virtually an impossibility for the individual believer since Christ has already absorbed God's righteous judgment on our behalf. Cf. the critique of G.C. Berkouwer in his great study of Barth, *The Triumph of Grace in the Theology of Karl Barth* (Grand Rapids, Mich.: Eerdmans, 1956), chapter 4, "The Triumph of Election."

12. G.C. Berkouwer, *Divine Election* (Grand Rapids, Mich.: Eerdmans, 1960),

pp. 213–14. Criticisms of Calvin's doctrine of double predestination are nothing new (see, for example, J.K.S. Reid's long introduction to Calvin's *Concerning the Eternal Predestination of God,* cited above, and the critique by an English evangelical, Francis Davidson, *Pauline Predestination* [London: Tyndale Press, 1946], pp. 32ff.).

Recently, critiques have been coming from conservative Dutch scholars like Berkouwer, A.D.R. Polman, and Herman Ridderbos, and Christian Reformed scholars like the late James Daane (who taught at Fuller Seminary until his retirement in 1979) and Harry Boer (retired missionary-theologian). See Daane's *The Freedom of God: A Study of Election and Pulpit* (Grand Rapids, Mich.: Eerdmans, 1973), in which he does not directly criticize Calvin but, in effect, rejects several aspects of his position.

Boer, on the other hand, has recently challenged the scriptural basis of the doctrine of reprobation as expressed in the *Canons of Dort.* See his "gravamen" (literally, "heavy objection") and the committee response in the *Agenda* for the 1980 Christian Reformed General synod. His latest book takes up this theme again in greater depth: *The Doctrine of Reprobation in the Christian Reformed Church* (Grand Rapids, Mich.: Eerdmans, 1983).

Calvin and the *Canons of Dort* find an able defender, however, in Professor Fred Klooster of Calvin Seminary. See his article in *The Banner* (November 23, 1979, pp. 8-12), "Predestination—A Calvinistic Note," which originally appeared in a symposium, *Perspectives on Evangelical Theology,* ed. Kenneth Kantzer and Stanley Gundry (Grand Rapids, Mich.: Baker Book House, 1979). See also the sympathetic treatment of election and reprobation (in the *Canons of Dort*) by the new systematic theologian at Calvin Seminary, Cornelius Plantinga, in his study of Reformed confessions, *A Place to Stand* (Grand Rapids, Mich.: Board of Publications of the Christian Reformed Church, 1979), chapter 28.

In the Reformed Church in America, Dr. Eugene Heideman suggests that there has been a movement away "from predestination to eschatology," but he provides practically no substantiation for this thesis. See his essay, "Theology," in *Piety and Patriotism (1776-1976),* ed. James W. Van Hoeven (Grand Rapids, Mich.: Eerdmans, 1976). Heideman may be speaking more for himself than the denomination as a whole, for he acknowledges in an appendix to *Our Song of Hope,* p. 87, "One can feel considerable tension between 'Our Song' and the Canons of Dort in the understanding of 'election.' . . ." He alludes to this "tension" in his commentary on Stanza 15—"Christ Elects His Church"—where he stresses the corporate rather than the individual nature of election (pp. 59-60).

13. Charles Williams, *The Descent of the Dove: The History of the Holy Spirit in the Church* (New York: Meridian Living Age Books, 1956), p. 191.

Williams, an English Anglican layman, was a friend and mentor to a number of distinguished writers, such as C.S. Lewis and J.R.R. Tolkien.

14. Osterhaven, *The Spirit of the Reformed Tradition,* p. 102. "When election is made into an isolated subject, is one-sidedly applied to the individual and his eternal destiny, and no longer is confessed but intellectually analyzed, it evokes a series of questions that are absolutely unanswerable because they are out of the covenant order. . ." (Berkhof, *Christian Faith,* p. 480).

15. Jonathan Edwards, *Works,* vol. 8, part 3, cited by G. Fackre in *The Rainbow Sign: Christian Futurity* (Grand Rapids, Mich.: Eerdmans, 1969), p. 61.

16. James I. Packer, *Evangelism and the Sovereignty of God* (Chicago: InterVarsity Press, 1967), p. 10.

17. "More than any other doctrine of Scripture, the doctrine of election throws into relief the absolute priority of divine grace. Election itself is God's sovereignty in terms of grace" (Philip E. Hughes, *But For the Grace of God: Divine Initiative and Human Need* [London: Hodder and Stoughton, 1964], p. 87).

18. "As by the most wise counsel of God the doctrine of divine election was preached by the Prophets, Christ himself, and the Apostles . . . so likewise today for the glory of God's holy name *and the life-giving comfort of his people,* it must be set forth in the Church of God . . ." (*Canons of Dort,* Article 14, emphasis mine. Cf. Article 6 and III.24.3-6).

Chapter Seven

1. One of G.C. Berkouwer's "Studies in Dogmatics." The title of the book is simply *Sin* (Grand Rapids, Mich.: Eerdmans, 1971).

A typical, traditional Calvinist view—but by an American Presbyterian of a past generation—is that by William G.T. Shedd:

> If the church and the ministry of the present day need any one thing more than another, it is profound views of sin; and if the current theology of the day is lacking in any one thing, it is in that thorough-going, that truly philosophic, and at the same time, truly edifying theory of sin, which runs like a strong muscular cord through all the soundest theology of the church.

(Shedd, *Theological Essays,* p. 264: cited by Thomas M. Gregory, "The Presbyterian Doctrine of Total Depravity," in *Soli Deo Gloria: Essays in Reformed Theology* [Festschrift for John H. Gerstner], ed. R.C. Sproul [Philadelphia: Presbyterian and Reformed Publishing Co., 1976], p. 36.)

2. Karl Menninger, *Whatever Became of Sin?* (New York: Hawthorn Books, 1973). Dr. Menninger is one of the founders of a psychiatric center in

Topeka, Kansas. The response to this volume was almost universally positive, both by theologians and by figures as diverse as Arnold Toynbee and Ann Landers.

3. Calvinism is given more credit than it deserves for being the progenitor or promoter of capitalism. This was the thesis of the famous economist Max Weber, and also R.H. Tawney. See *Protestantism and Capitalism: The Weber Thesis and Its Critics,* ed. Robert W. Green (Boston: D.C. Heath and Co., 1959).

4. H. Richard Neibuhr, *Christ and Culture* (New York: Harper & Brothers, 1951), chapter 6. Cf. Henry R. Van Til, *The Calvinistic Concept of Culture* (Philadelphia: The Presbyterian and Reformed Publishing Co., 1959).

5. Calvin does speak occasionally of man's depravity, but, as far as I know, does not use the phrase "total depravity," although the idea is there. for example, Take, this passage from his treatise "On Reforming the Church": "Man's whole nature is so imbued with depravity, that of himself he possesses no ability to act aright" (*Calvin: Theological Treatises,* ed. J.K.S. Reid [Philadelphia: Westminster Press, 1954], p. 198). For a closer analysis of Calvin's view of "total depravity," see Gregory, "The Presbyterian Doctrine of Total Depravity," pp. 41ff.

6. See note at bottom p. 27.

7. Chapter III-IV, Article 3, *Liturgy and Psalms,* p. 505.

8. Note that also in the *Westminster Confession* there is no suggestion that man is incapable of doing anything worthwhile. The language of VI,4—"utterly indisposed . . . to all good"—should be read in the context of IX,3—"wholly lost all ability of will *to any spiritual good accompanying* salvation." The last phrase is crucial. The implication is that, like Calvin, the Westminster fathers are not denying man's ability to do good things on the horizontal level, i.e., in realms other than our salvation. More recent hyper-Calvinists such as Herman Hoeksema (founder of the Protestant Reformed denomination) and Cornelius Van Til go even further in denying that man is capable of any good, even on the horizontal level.

9. In Reformed circles one hears more often of "common" grace in contrast to God's "special," i.e., redemptive, grace. On the debate about common grace in Dutch-American Calvinist circles, see H. Kuiper, *Calvin on Common Grace* (Grand Rapids, Mich.: Eerdmans, 1930).

10. *The Canons of Dort,* like Calvin, refer rather often to "the light of nature" which remains in a man in a small measure even after the fall (Chapter III-IV, Articles 4-7). The Canons, however, seem somewhat more pessimistic than Calvin when they say that "in various ways" natural man "far more often *wholly* pollutes this light, whatever its character . . ." (Chapter III-IV, Article 4, emphasis mine).

11. The *Second Helvetic Confession* echoes Calvin's view in a section entitled "Understanding the Arts" (which follows a discussion of sin entitled "Man Is Not Capable of Good Per Se"):

For God in his mercy has permitted the powers of the intellect to remain, though differing greatly from what was in man before the fall. God commands us to cultivate our natural talents, and meanwhile adds both gifts and success. And it is obvious we make no progress in all the arts without God's blessing. In any case, the Scripture traces all the arts to God; and indeed, the heathen trace the origin of the arts to the gods who invented them. (Cochrane, *Reformed Confessions,* p. 238)

12. Will Durant, *The Reformation* (New York: Simon and Schuster, 1957), p. 465.
13. Niebuhr, *Christ and Culture,* p. 214.
14. Henry Petersen, *The Canons of Dort: A Study Guide* (Grand Rapids, Mich.: Baker Book House, 1968), p. 45.
15. Plantinga, *A Place to Stand,* pp. 148-49.
16. This might appear to contradict the *Heidelberg Catechism,* which affirms that we are "so perverted that we are altogether unable to do good and are prone to do evil" (Q. 8); but the reference is, I believe, to moral good.
17. Berkouwer, *Sin,* p. 547.
18. This point is made by H.N. Ridderbos in his *Commentary on Romans,* cited in Berkouwer, *Sin,* p. 549, note 7.
19. Anthony H. Hoekema, *The Christian Looks at Himself* (Grand Rapids, Mich.: Eerdmans, 1975), p. 48. This is a refreshing treatment of the Christian self-image, based on traditional Reformed theology combined with recent psychological insights.
20. For Calvin's view of man see also G.C. Berkouwer, *Man: The Image of God* (Grand Rapids, Mich.: Eerdmans, 1962), and also T.F. Torrance, *Calvin's Doctrine of Man* (London: Lutterworth Press, 1949). Torrance's thesis is that with Calvin the doctrine of the corruption of man is a corollary of the doctrine of grace.

Chapter Eight

1. For a balanced discussion of this incident see Francois Wendel, *Calvin: Origins and Development of His Religious Thought* (New York: Harper and Row, 1963), pp. 93ff.
2. Friedrich Brunstad, *Theologie der lutherischen Bekenntnisschriften* (Gutersloh: C. Bertelsmann, 1951), pp. 79-80.
3. The best treatment of this subject is by the French Calvin scholar Richard Stauffer, in his little book, *The Humanness of Calvin* (Nashville: Abingdon Press, 1971).
4. N.H.G. Robinson, *The Groundwork of Christian Ethics* (Grand Rapids, Mich.: Eerdmans, 1971), p. 18; cf. pp. 19, 22.
5. Hesselink, *Calvin: Concept and Use of the Law* (The University of Basel, Switzerland, 1961) Copies are in the Western and Calvin Seminary,

libraries in Basel University Library, and in the British Library Lending Division.

6. Cf. the Sasse quote in Osterhaven, *Spirit*, p. 133.

7. Cf. Calvin's commentary on the *Last Four Books of Moses*, vols. 2 and 3, in which he harmonizes all of the Mosaic legislation around the Ten Commandments.

8. In his rules for interpreting the Decalogue in the *Institutes*, II.8.6-12, note how the majority of his references come from the Sermon on the Mount.

9. See his commentaries on 2 Corinthians 3:16-17 and Romans 10:4.

10. Commentary on Romans 10:4; cf. II.7.1,2. Law, here, obviously means more than simply the Ten Commandments. In fact, it is closer to being the equivalent of the Old Testament—and yet is to be distinguished from the gospel, which is also found in the Old Testament.

11. See Paul Jewett, *The Lord's Day: A Theological Guide to the Christian Day of Worship* (Grand Rapids, Mich.: Eerdmans, 1971), pp. 77-78, 102-6.

12. See Holmes Rolston III, *John Calvin versus the Westminster Confession* (Richmond, Va.: John Knox Press, 1972). His thesis is that federal theology (a special type of covenant theology which stressed a covenant of works), which finds expression in the *Westminster Confession,* is the culprit. See especially pp. 11ff. and 90ff.

13. See Calvin's beautiful discussion of the preface to the Decalogue in II.8.13-15. Note his reasoning that God tries to elicit our faithfulness and obedience not so much by his authority and majesty as by his "sweetness" and "kindness." Here too Calvin speaks eloquently of God as the "author of our freedom" who would "lead us into the Kingdom of freedom."

14. This is another theme of Calvin's. On the place of the law in the *Heidelberg Catechism*, see Osterhaven, *Spirit*, pp. 134-37, and my section in *Guilt, Grace, and Gratitude*, ed. Donald J. Bruggink (New York: The Half Moon Press, 1963), pp. 169f., 194-208.

15. Paul Wernle, *Calvin* (Tubingen: Mohr, 1919), p. 131.

16. Calvin spells this out in a way that will surprise most people in the next section (III.19.9).

Chapter Nine

1. See Walther Eichrodt's monumental *Theology of the Old Testament* (Philadelphia: Westminster Press, vol. 1, 1961; vol. 2, 1967). Cf. the pioneering work of George Mendenhall, *Law and Covenant in Israel and the Far East* (Pittsburgh: The Biblical Colloquium, 1955), and his essay, "Covenant," in *The Interpreter's Dictionary of the Bible*, vol. 1, ed. G.A. Buttrick (Nashville: Abingdon Press, 1962). For a more comprehensive theological treatment see Jacob Jocz, *The Covenant: A Theology of Human Destiny* (Grand Rapids, Mich.: Eerdmans, 1968).

2. The great Puritan scholar, Perry Miller, errs seriously in his judgment that

"Luther and Calvin made hardly mention of the covenant and the great confessions of sixteenth-century Protestantism avoided it entirely" (*Errand into the Wilderness* [Cambridge, Mass.: Harvard University Press, 1956, Harper Torchbook edition 1964], p. 60). Miller may be right about Luther and the sixteenth-century confessions, but Osterhaven has demonstrated convincingly that this is not true of Calvin. See Osterhaven's essay, "Calvin on the Covenant," in the *Reformed Review*, Spring 1980, and reprinted in *A Covenant Challenge to Our Broken World*, ed. Allen O. Miller, published by Caribbean and North American Area Council of the World Council of Churches (Atlanta: Darby Printing Co., 1982).

3. Covenant theology was also taken up in earnest in the early seventeenth century by the English Puritans. One of their leading covenant theologians was William Ames (1576-1633), who was also one of Coccejus' teachers. Ames's influential *Marrow of Theology* is available in English, ed. John Dykstra (Boston: Pilgrim Press, 1968).

4. See note 7 below.

5. See Kuyper's *Lectures on Calvinism*, originally given in 1898 (Grand Rapids, Mich.: Eerdmans, 1931/53).

6. March, 1977, pp. 20ff. George Groen is the superintendent of the Ontario, California, Christian School Association.

7. Particularly intriguing—and unfortunate—has been the use (or misuse) of Abraham Kuyper's theology, especially his idea of "sphere-sovereignty," by some South African Calvinists. See John W. De Gruchy, "Bonhoeffer, Calvinism and Christian Civil Disobedience in South Africa," *Scottish Journal of Theology* 34 (1981), pp. 248ff.

8. "Federal" in this phrase derives from the Latin *foedus*, meaning a "covenant" or "alliance."

9. Rolston, *John Calvin versus the Westminster Confession*, chapter 7, "The Westminster Confession and Covenant Theology." Rolston is overly zealous in making his point, but this chapter does provide a revealing overview of how much covenant theology influenced the Westminster divines. Cf. Torrance, *The School of Faith*, pp. lxiiiff. Unlike Rolston, Torrance recognizes some of the benefits of covenant theology as well as its dangers.

10. (Grand Rapids, Mich.: Eerdmans, 1949). See Part II, chapter 4. It is significant that in the section, "The Scriptural Foundation for the Doctrine of the Covenant of Works" (pp. 213f.), no texts are cited!

11. See especially Albertus Pieters' T.V. Moore Lectures given at San Francisco Theological Seminary in 1949, *The Seed of Abraham* (Grand Rapids, Mich.: Eerdmans, 1950). This was recently reprinted in a special limited edition in 1978. Cf. the review article of this book by Mark J. Bergsma in the *Reformed Review* (Autumn 1979).

12. John Murray, *The Covenant of Grace* (London: Tyndale Press, 1953).

13. Murray, *Covenant*, pp. 30-31.

14. Berkhof, *Christian Faith,* p. 536. Berkhof discusses the significance of the covenant in various contexts in his dogmatics. In speaking of eternal life, he writes: "From the intimate oneness of the Father and the Son we can tell what God's covenant purpose is. Our expectation of the future is that, on account of Christ and following after him we shall share in God's sphere of life. That is a staggering and unimaginable perspective."

15. This spirit was always a temptation to Jews as well, since they were very conscious of themselves as being a "people of the covenant." For a contemporary analysis of this problem by a Jewish scholar see "The Covenant Concept—Particularistic, Pluralistic, or Futuristic?" by Jacob B. Agus in *Journal of Ecumenical Studies* 18 (Spring 1981), pp. 217ff.

16. Eichrodt, *Theology,* p. 29.

17. The theme of the symposium is the title of the book, *A Covenant Challenge to Our Broken World,* referred to above in note 2. Other contributors, not as well known internationally, but representing the Reformed and Christian Reformed Churches, are John W. Beardslee III, Fred H. Klooster, Hugh A. Koops, and M. Eugene Osterhaven.

18. For this emphasis I am indebted to Harry Boer's important little book, *That My House May Be Filled* (Grand Rapids, Mich.: Eerdmans, 1957), chapter 7. This has been reiterated by Robert Recker, professor of missiology at Calvin Theological Seminary, in an article "Abraham—A Walking Blessing of God," in *The Banner,* March 18, 1977, p. 8. He makes his point forthrightly:

> We commonly hear the misconception expressed that God's special relationship with Israel in the Old Testament era was opposed to the New Testament concept of mission. People who say this think of the covenantal emphasis as an accent on self-centeredness, or at least as a preoccupation with their own existence, protection and development.
> This view of the role of the covenant is a faulty one.

Similarly, Jack Rogers of Fuller Theological Seminary in an address, "The Three C's of Presbyterianism," in *The Presbyterian Communique,* (Spring 1982), pp. 6-7: He says that 1) that Presbyterians are a covenant people who make confession of their faith and 2) that Presbyterians are also a covenant people who live out their faith according to a constitution. His third point is "Presbyterians are a covenant people who act out their faith connectionally." By "connectionally" Rogers means sharing with others in mission.

Chapter Ten

1. See Timothy Smith, *Revivalism and Social Reform* (Nashville: Abingdon Press, 1957); and Sherwood Wirt, *The Social Conscience of the Evan-*

gelical (New York: Harper & Row, 1968), pp. 33-36.

2. Besides the Moral Majority there are similar groups such as Christian Voice and Religious Roundtable, the latter being directed by a Baptist layman, Ed McAteer of Memphis. For comprehensive treatments of this phenomenon see Robert E. Webber, *The Moral Majority: Right or Wrong?* (Westchester, Ill.: Cornerstone Books, 1981); and Samuel S. Hill and Dennis E. Owen, *The New Religious Right in America* (Nashville: Abingdon Press, 1982). Webber is a professor at Wheaton College. Hill and Owen teach at the University of Florida. Cf. *Theology Today* 39 (January 1983), which contains reviews of five books about the Moral Majority and the New Right.

For a brief, balanced appraisal from an evangelical, Reformed perspective see Richard Mouw's article, "Assessing the Moral Majority," in the *Reformed Journal* 31 (June 1981). My own views are expressed briefly in a "Response" to a paper by Dale Vree, editor of the *New Oxford Review,* entitled "Ideology Versus Theology: Case Studies of Liberation Theology and the Christian New Right," both in *Christianity Confronts Modernity,* ed. Peter Williamson and Kevin Perrotta (Ann Arbor, Mich.: Servant Books, 1981), pp. 79ff.

3. Called the "King Midas of the New Right" because of his ability to raise millions for right-wing causes, Richard Viguerie is one of the leading political figures in the new movement. He is Roman Catholic, as is one of his cohorts, Paul Weyrich. Another leader, Howard Phillips, is Jewish.

4. Of course, liberal scholars and politicians are alarmed by the New Right, but Billy Graham is also concerned about the way the Moral Majority has lined up with the political right. See Marguerite Michaels, "Billy Graham Challenges the Moral Majority," *Parade* (February 1, 1981), pp. 5-7.

5. See Paul Ramsey, *Who Speaks for the Church?* (Nashville: Abingdon Press, 1967).

6. It is noteworthy that the first article in the postwar (1950) confession of the Dutch Reformed Church is "God, Our King." See *Foundations and Perspectives of Confession,* p. 11; cf. p. 31.

7. On this theme, see two outstanding studies by Reformed biblical scholars—the one a prize-winning work by John Bright, distinguished emeritus professor of Old Testament at Union Theological Seminary in Richmond, Virginia, *The Kingdom of God: The Biblical Concept and Its Meaning for the Church* (Nashville: Abingdon Press, 1955); the other the magisterial study of this theme by the great Dutch New Testament scholar from Kampen, Herman Ridderbos, *The Coming of the Kingdom* (Philadelphia: The Presbyterian and Reformed Publishing Co., 1962).

"It may be rightly said that the whole of the preaching of Jesus Christ and his apostles is concerned with the kingdom of God, and that in Jesus Christ's proclamation of the kingdom we are face to face with the specific form of expression of the whole of his revelation of God" (Ibid., p. xi).

8. Grand Rapids, Mich.: Eerdmans, 1980.

9. Ibid., p. 2.

10. Ibid., p. 67.

11. See the *Reformed Review* 26, Winter 1973, devoted to van Ruler. He was a pastor for many years and then taught theology at the University of Utrecht until his death in 1970.

12. See my essay, "The Catholic Character of Calvin's Life and Work," *Reformed Review* 19, December 1965. Cf. André Bieler, *The Social Humanism of Calvin* (Richmond, Va.: John Knox Press, 1964); and W. Fred Graham, *The Constructive Revolutionary: John Calvin and His Socio-Economic Impact* (Richmond: John Knox Press, 1971).

13. There are a host of popular studies of these so-called five points of Calvinism. Representative are Ben A. Warburton, *Calvinism: Its History, Basic Principles, Its Fruits . . .* (Grand Rapids, Mich.: Eerdmans, 1955); Petersen, *The Canons of Dort*; David N. Steele and Curtis C. Thomas, *The Five Points of Calvinism: Defined, Defended, Documented* (Philadelphia: Presbyterian and Reformed Publishing Co., 1963); Duane Edward Spender, *TULIP: The Five Points of Calvinism in the Light of Scripture* (Grand Rapids, Mich.: Baker Book House, 1979). A scholarly series of essays on the *Synod of Dort* and the theological issues involved was published by the Reformed Fellowship, Inc., in Grand Rapids in 1968— *Crisis in the Reformed Churches: Essays in Commemoration of the Great Synod of Dort, 1618-1619.*

14. New York: Holt, Rinehart and Winston, 1963, translated from the German edition, *Vom Heiligung in der Kunst.*

15. One of the foremost theological scholars in the field of church architecture is Donald J. Bruggink, professor of church history at Western Theological Seminary. See his two works in this field: *Christ and Architecture*, in collaboration with Carl Droppers (Grand Rapids, Mich.: Eerdmans, 1965); and *When Faith Takes Form* (Grand Rapids, Mich.: Eerdmans, 1971).

16. This should not be taken to suggest that a theological interest in the arts is limited to the Reformed tradition. See, for example, *Theology and Contemporary Art Forms* by John P. Newport, professor of religion at Southwestern Baptist Seminary in Fort Worth, Texas (Waco, Texas: Word Books, 1970). Even here, however, it is noted in the dust jacket that his work in this area was initiated and stimulated during his graduate study at the University of Edinburgh. Cf. *Theology and the Arts* by David Baily Harned (Philadelphia: Westminster Press, 1966). Harned is president of Allegheny College, Meadville, Pa. One should not overlook the widely read book in this area by the Dutch scholar, Hans Rookmaaker, *Modern Art and the Death of a Culture* (Downers Grove, Ill.: InterVarsity Press, 1970).

17. Toronto: Tuppence Press, 1980.

18. Grand Rapids, Mich.: Eerdmans, 1980. Cf. his related, more philosophically oriented book, *Works and Worlds of Art* (New York: Oxford University Press, 1980).

19. Van Til, *The Calvinistic Concept of Culture*, p. 3. Cf. Wolterstorff, *Art in Action*, p. 177.

20. Seerveld, *Rainbows*, p. 9.

21. Edinburgh: The Handsel Press, and Grand Rapids, Mich.: Eerdmans, 1980.

22. Ibid., pp. 45-46.

23. See T.G. Homes, "*Deus Ludens*: Christianity and Culture in the Theology of A.A. van Ruler," *Reformed Review*, Winter 1973.

24. See especially the following stanzas in *Our Song of Hope*: 5-8, 10-11, 18-19. Note the frequency and linkage of references to Spirit and the world, nations, government(s), knowledge, and research.

25. See his *Theological Science* (London: Oxford University Press, 1969); *Space, Time and Incarnation* (London: Oxford University Press, 1969); and *Reality and Evangelical Theology* (Philadelphia: Westminster Press, 1982).

26. Torrance, *Reality and Evangelical Theology*, p. 27.

27. Ibid., p. 21.

28. New York: Harper & Row, 1967, pp. 23, 28, 112. The British version (London: SCM Press, 1968) has the title *Theology for a New World*. Cf. my article-review, "An American Theology," in the *Reformed Review* 23 (Summer 1970).

29. Gordon J. Spykman, "Sphere-Sovereignty in Calvin and the Calvinist Tradition," in *Exploring the Heritage of John Calvin*, ed. David E. Holwerda (Grand Rapids, Mich.: Baker Book House, 1976), p. 164. For a contrasting, Baptist approach, see Robert Duncan Culver's *Toward a Biblical View of Civil Government* (Chicago: Moody Press, 1975).

Chapter Eleven

1. Lewis Mudge, *One Church: Catholic and Reformed* (Philadelphia: Westminster Press, 1963), p. 63.

2. See chapter 5, especially pp. 39f.

3. See Battles, *Piety*, and Richard, *Spirituality*.

4. He defined piety as "that reverence joined with the love of God which the knowledge of his benefits induces" (I.2.1). The argument is circular, for earlier he had said that, "properly speaking, God is [not] known where there is no religion or piety" (I.2.1). Cf. I.4.1; I.5.4; II.6.4 (here and occasionally elsewhere *pietas* is translated by Battles as "godliness" rather than "piety").

5. Ford Lewis Battles's, *John Calvin: Catechism 1538*, trans. and annotated by Ford Lewis Battles (Pittsburgh: Pittsburgh Theological Seminary, 1972), p. 17. Battles' translation is based on the Latin edition, whereas Paul T.

Fuhrman based his translation, entitled *Instruction in Faith* (Philadelphia: Westminster Press, 1949), on the 1537 French edition.

Later, in the *Institutes,* we find similar words in one of his many definitions of faith: "For the Word of God is not received by faith if it flits about on top of the brain, but when it takes root in the depth of the *heart* that it may be an invincible defense . . ." (II.3.36). Almost identical words are used to describe the knowledge of God in I.5.9. (Emphasis here and elsewhere is mine.)

6. Battles, *Catechism,* p. 19. Also, faith "is a firm and staunch confidence of the *heart* by which we securely repose in God's mercy promised us through the Gospel," ibid., p. 18. Cf. III.2.8.

7. James W. Jones puts his finger on the motivation for this emphasis, namely, Calvin's constant quest for assurance and certainty in matters of faith. "For Calvin, authority lies in something being confirmed as authoritative in the heart of the individual. . . . The mind cannot give certainty, Calvin says, because its knowledge always comes through the senses and is therefore subject to doubt. The will can give no certainty either for it is dependent upon the mind. But the heart is the seat of certainty and assurance for Calvin" (*The Spirit and the World* [New York: Hawthorn Books, 1975], p. 131).

Confirmation of this point is seen in passages like this one (III.2.36): "It is harder for the *heart* to be furnished with assurance than for the *mind* to be endowed with thought. The Spirit accordingly serves as a seal, to seal up in our *hearts* those very promises the certainty of which it has previously impressed upon our minds; and takes the place of a guarantee to confirm and establish them." Calvin then cites Ephesians 1:13-14; 2 Corinthians 1:22; and 2 Corinthians 5:5 to illustrate and confirm this point.

8. One should also note that faith is based on the promise of God's benevolence, mercy, and grace manifested to us in Christ. Cf. III.2.7,38.

9. The great Princeton scholar of a past era, B.B. Warfield, was the first to so describe Calvin. See *Calvin and Augustine* (Philadelphia: Presbyterian and Reformed Publishing Co., 1956), pp. 21-24, 107. This was later repeated by John Mackay, former president of Princeton Seminary; Bernard Ramm, well-known evangelical Baptist theologian; and Werner Krusche, now an East German Lutheran bishop, in his magisterial study, *Das Wirken des Heiligen Geistes nach Calvin* (Göttingen: Vandenhoeck and Ruprecht, 1957), p. 12. Even prior to B.B. Warfield, Abraham Kuyper had written, "The doctrine of the Holy Spirit is a gift from John Calvin to the Church of Christ" (*The Work of the Holy Spirit* [Grand Rapids, Mich.: Eerdmans, 1946. The original English edition appeared in 1900]).

10. Some of the following material is an adaptation of part of a lecture I gave at a Western Seminary Fall Institute (1974) on the theme, "The Holy Spirit and Charismatic Theology." My lecture was entitled, "The Charismatic Movement and the Reformed Tradition." It appears along with the other

addresses given at that Institute in *Reformed Review* 28, Spring 1975, pp. 147ff. Cf. an earlier essay, "Charismatic Theology and the New Testament," by Richard C. Oudersluys, emeritus professor of New Testament at Western Seminary, in the *Reformed Review* 28, Autumn 1974.

11. Bernard Ramm provides an excellent treatment of Calvin's approach and the broader issues involved in his book, *The Witness of the Spirit: An Essay on the Contemporary Relevance of the Internal Witness of the Holy Spirit* (Grand Rapids, Mich.: Eerdmans, 1959), especially pp. 11ff.

12. Of the various words which can be used to describe the work of the exalted Christ in the life of believers—"vocation," "conversion," "justification," "sanctification"—Hendrikus Berkhof believes that "the word which best expresses the unity and the totality of the Spirit's work is the word 'regeneration'" (*The Doctrine of the Holy Spirit* [Richmond, Va.: John Knox Press, 1964/1977], p. 69.

13. "That joining together of Head and members, that indwelling of Christ in our hearts—in short that mystical union—are accorded by us the highest degree of importance, so that Christ, having been made ours, makes us sharers with him in the gifts with which he has been endowed" (III.11.10). Calvin warns, however, against any confusing of Christ's essence with ours (III.11.5).

14. Cf. III.2.24: "Not only does he [Christ] cleave to us by an indivisible bond of fellowship, but with a wonderful communion (*societas*) day by day, he grows more and more into one body with us, until he becomes completely one with us."

    The best discussions of this in English are in Wendel's *Calvin*, pp. 234ff., and Smedes, *All Things*, pp. 171ff.: "If John Calvin can be called the theologian of the Spirit, he can also be called the theologian of the indwelling Christ."

15. See Lycurgus M. Starkey, Jr., *The Work of the Holy Spirit: A Study in Wesleyan Theology* (New York/Nashville: Abingdon Press, 1962). See especially pp. 126f., 135ff., where Starkey finds more similiarities between Wesley and Calvin than Wesley and Luther.

16. On this, see the perceptive comments of Barth in *Church Dogmatics*, IV, 2, pp. 509f.

17. He uses a variety of expressions in the *Institutes* (and elsewhere): "Under the Spirit's guidance" (I.17.3, III.20.5), "ruled by the Holy Spirit" (I.18.2, cf. III.1.3), "governs them by his Spirit" (IV.8.13). Several are brought together in this passage: "The Lord by his Spirit directs, bends, and governs our heart and reigns in it as in his own possession" (II.3.10).

18. Berkhof, *Doctrine of the Holy Spirit*, p. 22.

19. Kilian McDonnell, *John Calvin, the Church and the Eucharist* (Princeton: Princeton University Press, 1967), p. 183.

20. This is the thesis of Joseph Bohatec, the Czech-Austrian Calvin scholar of a

past generation, in his massive study, *Calvins Lehre von Staat und Kirche* (Breslau: M. and H. Marcus, 1937), pp. 267f.

21. Ibid., pp. 422-43. Cf. McDonnell, *Calvin,* p. 183.

22. On the specific role of the Holy Spirit in infant baptism, see IV.16.17, 18; in the Lord's Supper, see IV.4.17.

23. Some would maintain that the most able German theologian of the nineteenth century was Friedrich Schleiermacher, who happened to be Reformed but is sometimes hailed as "the father of liberalism." He has a doctrine of the Spirit which in one respect—the communal emphasis—has something to offer us today. So, in any case, says James Jones in *The Spirit and the World,* pp. 138ff.

24. See M. Eugene Osterhaven, "The Experiential Theology of Early Dutch Calvinism," *Reformed Review* 27 (Spring 1974), pp. 180ff. Cf. F. Ernest Stoeffler, *The Rise of Evangelical Pietism* (Leiden: E.J. Brill, 1965).

25. See the superb dissertation by James Tanis, *Dutch Calvinistic Pietism in the Middle Colonies: A Study in the Life and Theology of Theodorus Jacobus Frelinghuysen* (The Hague: Martinus Nijhoff, 1967).

26. Two, whose works have been reprinted by the Banner of Truth Publishers are James Buchanan's *The Office and Work of the Holy Spirit* (1843, Reprint 1966), and Octavius Winslow's *The Work of the Holy Spirit* (1840, Reprint 1972). There have also been reprints of some of the works of the earlier English Puritan, John Owen, who wrote three works on the Holy Spirit, published in 1674, 1682, and 1693.

27. Eerdmans reprinted it in 1946.

28. O. Noordmans, *Das Evangelium des Geistes* (Zurich: EVZ Verlag, 1960).

29. See the special issue of *Reformed Review* 26 (Winter 1973), devoted to his theology.

30. Philadelphia: Westminster Press, 1957; revised edition 1965. Hendry was born and reared in Scotland but taught most of his career at Princeton Theological Seminary.

31. Philadelphia: Westminster Press, 1959. Come taught theology for many years at San Francisco Theological Seminary and, later, was its president until his retirement in 1981.

32. It is striking that, in the index to the Library of Christian Classics edition of the *Institutes,* under "Holy Spirit" there is no reference either to gifts or fruit of the Spirit. There is a passing reference to the gifts in connection with 1 Corinthians 12:28. There Calvin discounts "powers, the gift of healing and interpretation" as being "temporary" and hence not worth "tarrying over them" (IV.3.8). In the *Institutes* there are many references to 1 Corinthians 14:40: "All things should be done decently and in order," but none to 14:39: "So, my brethren, earnestly desire to prophesy, and do not forbid speaking in tongues." In his commentary on this passage he simply says Paul "is pointing out that prophecy is worth aspiring to

earnestly and eagerly, on the part of all. At the same time he urges them not to begrudge the rarer gifts of *tongues* to others, for it is not to be sought after so much" (*Calvin's New Testament Commentaries—1 Corinthians*, trans. John W. Fraser [Grand Rapids, Mich.: Eerdmans, 1960], p. 310).

The disinterest, if not the distaste of the reformers for speaking in tongues, prophesying, etc., may be partially explained by their fear of and aversion to the "enthusiasts" (*Schwaermer*) and "fanatics" such as the Anabaptists and more radical, left-wing reformers. On the broader issue, see the essay by Paul Elbert, "Calvin and the Spiritual Gifts," in *Journal of the Evangelical Theological Society* 22 (September 1979), pp. 235ff.; and Leonard Sweetman, Jr., "The Gift of the Spirit: A Study of Calvin's Comments on 1 Corinthians 12:8-10, 28; Romans 12:6-8; Ephesians 4:11," in *Exploring the Heritage of John Calvin*, pp. 273ff. Both essays are thorough and perceptive.

33. Warfield is not as well known as his predecessors in the theology chair at Princeton Seminary, Charles Hodge and his son A.A. Hodge, whom Warfield succeeded in 1887. But his works have endured and are read more today than those of both of the Hodges. His collected works were published posthumously by Oxford University Press (1929-1932) and have recently been reprinted by Baker Book House, Grand Rapids. In the 1950s several of his major works were reprinted by the Presbyterian and Reformed Publishing Co. in Philadelphia.

34. Warfield, *Miracles* (Grand Rapids, Mich.: Eerdmans), pp. 5-6; cf. pp. 21ff.

Much of the book is given over to countering a view popular in certain Protestant circles at that time, namely, that miracles continued for a while— up to two centuries—after the apostolic period and then slowly died out.

35. See his *What About Tongue Speaking?* (Grand Rapids, Mich.: Eerdmans, 1966/1973).

36. See his *Perspectives on Pentecost: New Testament Teaching on the Gifts of the Holy Spirit* (Grand Rapids, Mich.: Baker Book House, 1979).

37. Hoekema, *What About*, p. 128.

This is actually the view of Donald S. Metz, head of the department of religion at Bethany Nazarene College, but Hoekema agrees with it, as well as with the view of Stuart Bergsma, former superintendent of the Pine Rest Christian Hospital in Grand Rapids, whom Hoekema quotes as concluding, after evaluating a number of experiences of glossolalia, that they "can be psychologically explained" and are "not, in general, a 'spiritual' phenomenon," p. 129. Cf. pp. 105ff. where Hoekema repeats Warfield's thesis about special miraculous gifts being intended to authenticate the apostles and their preaching and therefore ceasing with them.

38. Gaffin, *Perspectives*, p. 102. The Warfield thesis is repeated on pp. 109, 117. In 1977, the editors of *The Presbyterian Journal*, a conservative, independent (but basically Southern Presbyterian) weekly published in Weaverville, N.C., challenged those who believe supernatural gifts have

ceased to prove their point from scripture. There were not many takers. But Robert E. Hays, a Presbyterian pastor from Clarendon, Arkansas, responded in the December 1977 issue that he believes that the Bible does indeed indicate that such gifts have ceased. His argument focuses on a distinction in 1 Corinthians 13:8, where Paul says that prophecies and knowledge "will pass away," but tongues "will cease," pp. 10-11. Other contributors in this issue take the opposite view.

39. Henry Pitney van Dunsen, "Caribbean Holiday," *Christian Century* (August 17, 1955), pp. 946f. Later, in 1960, he declared, "The Pentecostal movement . . . is a revolution comparable in importance with the establishment of the original church and with the Protestant Reformation," quoted by J. Rodman Williams, "The Upsurge of Pentecostalism," in *The Reformed World* 31 (December 1971), p. 340.

40. Lesslie Newbigin, *The Household of God* (New York: Friendship Press, 1953), pp. 95f, 122.

41. G.C. Berkouwer, *The Providence of God* (Grand Rapids, Mich.: Eerdmans, 1952), pp. 238, 242. Berkouwer is obviously thinking here of liberal, rather than more conservative, opponents.

42. Berkhof, *Doctrine,* p. 10.

43. Ibid., p. 11.

44. Ibid., p. 85.

45. The Presbyterian Church U.S. (Southern) produced a similar study, *The Person and Work of the Holy Spirit,* the following year (1971).

46. Ibid., p. 3.

47. Ibid., p. 46.

48. Ibid., p. 13.
    "A More Detailed Summary of Relevant Psychological Literature" is contained in Appendix B (pp. 47-55). Conclusion: "The subcommittee found no evidence of pathology in the movement. The movement was found to be dynamic, growing, and involving persons from practically every denomination, walk and station in life," p. 55.

49. Ibid., p. 45.

50. Frederick Dale Bruner, *A Theology of the Holy Spirit* (Grand Rapids, Mich.: Eerdmans, 1970), p. 14. Not all neo-Pentecostals believe that "Spirit-baptism" necessarily results in speaking in tongues, although it is usually considered an important confirmation of that experience. On this point see Anthony Hoekema, *Holy Spirit Baptism* (Grand Rapids, Mich.: Eerdmans, 1972), pp. 30ff.

51. This is a complicated matter which cannot be explored here. I can only refer readers to several key studies which elucidate and substantiate (I feel) this position. One should begin with the thorough, highly regarded study by the Scottish Presbyterian scholar James D.G. Dunn, *Baptism in the Holy Spirit* (London: SCM Press, 1970). Cf. Hoekema's *Holy Spirit Baptism,* cited above, and the smaller study by John R.W. Stott, *The*

Baptism and the Fullness of the Holy Spirit (Downers Grove, Ill.: InterVarsity Press, 1974). For a contrary view, ably argued, see Charles E. Hummel, *Fire in the Fireplace: Contemporary Charismatic Renewal* (Downers Grove, Ill.: InterVarsity Press (1978), especially pp. 185ff.

52. A small but growing number of Reformed Church ministers are active in the Presbyterian Charismatic Communion, 2245 N.W. 39th St., Oklahoma City, OK 73112.

53. A case in point is the sharp critique of Reformed Churches, *Not Reformed but Transformed*, by Peter Teerling, a charismatic leader in Western Michigan of Dutch-Canadian Christian Reformed background (Grand Rapids, Mich.: Logos Fellowship, 1973).

54. James I. Cook, "The Fruit of the Spirit in the Life of Believers," *Reformed Review* 28 (Spring 1975), p. 199.

> While not denying the gifts of the Spirit in the life of the church, Paul shifts his emphasis from gifts to fruit. Gifts, *charismata,* of the special kind encountered at Corinth are not mentioned by Paul in his correspondence with other churches. The Spirit is indeed the cause of the marvelous, but the most truly marvelous for Paul is the life that displays the qualities he describes as the fruit of the Spirit—the sanctified life!

Cf. the essay in the same issue by Richard C. Oudersluys, "The Purpose of Spiritual Gifts," pp. 212ff.

55. This distinction is used by John Stevens Kerr in his book, *The Fire Flares Anew: A Look at the New Pentecostalism* (Philadelphia: Fortress Press, 1974).

56. See the fine discussion of this issue in regard to the charismatic movement by Michael Green in his book *I Believe in the Holy Spirit* (Grand Rapids, Mich.: Eerdmans, 1975), pp. 209ff. Cf. M. Eugene Osterhaven's chapter, "John Calvin: Order and the Holy Spirit," in *The Faith of the Church: A Reformed Perspective on Its Historical Development* (Grand Rapids, Mich.: Eerdmans, 1982), pp. 162ff.

57. Even the great Dutch Reformed theologian Abraham Kuyper conceded as much in the closing words of the preface (pp. xi-xii) to his *The Work of the Holy Spirit*: "Even though we honor the Father and believe on the Son, how little do we live in the Holy Spirit! It even seems to us sometimes that for our sanctification *only,* the Holy Spirit is added accidentally to the great redemptive work."

Chapter Twelve

1. The Reformed Church in America has engaged seriously in merger negotiations several times but has always failed to ratify specific union

proposals. For this story see the book by Herman Harmelink III, *Ecumenism and the Reformed Church* (Grand Rapids, Mich.: Eerdmans, 1968). For current attitudes in the Christian Reformed Church toward possible reunion see the rather negative slant in the January 10, 1983, issue of *The Banner.*

2. John Mackay, *The Presbyterian Way of Life* (Englewood Cliffs, N.J.: Prentice-Hall, Inc., 1960), p. 213.

3. Harmelink, *Ecumenism,* p. 7.

4. On the sin of schism see IV.1.10-16.

5. It should be kept in mind that unity, according to the New Testament, does not mean some hidden, invisible unity of spirit or belief but also has concrete visible implications. As Herman Ridderbos, the great Dutch Reformed New Testament scholar, explains in *Paul: An Outline of His Theology* (Grand Rapids, Mich.: Eerdmans, 1975), p. 394:

> Because all believers together are one body in Christ, the dividedness of Christ is in conflict with its being, for Christ is not divided (1 Cor. 1:13). Nor can one restrict this unity to the sphere of what is invisible and hidden. Not only does the word "body" not denote an invisible but a visible mode of existence, but on the ground of being together in Christ Paul concludes the necessity of a visible, outward manifestation of unity as the body (cf. 1 Cor. 1:13; 12:12ff.; Rom 12:4, 5; Eph 4:15, 16, 25; Col 3:14, 15).

6. For Calvin's precise wording see IV.1.9 (and note 16 on page 1023 in the Library of Christian Classics edition concerning church discipline as a third mark).

7. These are the phrases Calvin uses in IV.1.10,12.

8. See the fine essay by Brian Gerrish, "John Calvin on Luther," in *Interpreters of Luther: Essays in Honor of Wilhelm Pauck,* ed. Jaroslav Pelikan (Philadelphia: Fortress Press, 1968), pp. 67-96. Cf. John T. McNeill, *Unitive Protestantism: The Ecumenical Spirit in Its Persistent Expression* (Richmond, Va.: John Knox Press, revised edition, 1964), pp. 185ff.

9. Letter of March 1540, cited in McNeill, *Unitive Protestantism,* pp. 184-85.

10. Bucer, the Strasbourg reformer, and Melanchthon could also qualify as prominent ecumenists of that era, but their influence was negligible during this period. See McNeill, *Unitive Protestantism,* pp. 195.

11. Ibid., p. 213.

12. Letter of April 1552 cited *ibid.,* p. 247, and in A. Mitchell Hunter, *The Teaching of Calvin* (London: James Clarke & Co., revised edition, 1950), p. 164. Cf. pp. 160ff. for other evidences of Calvin's concern for unity.

13. Hunter, *Teaching of Calvin,* p. 160.

Calvin played for high stakes. Had his ardent hopes been fulfilled, Protestantism would have taken the outlines of a church ecumenical and conciliar, in which the unity which was once attained on the monarchical principle of government at the cost of no little repression, under the papacy, would have been succeeded by a general communion under the government of a representative body expressive of the voluntary cohesion of the states, cities, and groups participating. Once established, this Protestant conciliar church of Europe might have chosen to employ the weapon of political coercion and thus have brought upon itself reproach, embarrassment, or ruin. On the other hand, if the resulting system had proved true to Calvin's idea of the communion of saints, it would have given expression on a grand scale to Christian fraternity, catholicity, and democracy, reversed the process of dissolution in the church, exhibited to the distracted states of Europe an impressive pattern of spontaneous unity, and rendered the last four centuries of Western history incomparably richer and happier than they have been. (McNeill, *Unitive Protestantism,* pp. 219-20)

14. *Liturgy and Psalms,* p. 449. Cf. Osterhaven, *Spirit of the Reformed Tradition,* pp. 39-44.

Commenting on a similar passage in the United Presbyterian *Book of Order* (33, 01), Dr. Jane D. Douglas, Presbyterian theologian and professor of church history at the School of Theology at Claremont, comments: "One distinctive mark of the Reformed or Presbyterian tradition is precisely this broad, ecumenical vision of the church of all times and places. We are not sectarians!" ("Reformed Distinctives," *Presbyterian Communique,* January/February 1981, p.1).

15. *Op cit., The Presbyterian Way,* pp. 212-13.

Chapter Thirteen

1. "One's testimony [as a denomination] must be clearly separated from seeking for one's own honor and also clearly separated from *our* cause, from *our* group, or from a transformation according to *our* model. Otherwise, the essence of being the church is violated. . . . When that happens the church and the confession have been secularized in a particular form of distinctive 'identity,' and the gospel is misunderstood" (Berkouwer, *The Church,* p. 73).

2. Doumergue, *Calvin,* vol. 4, p. 426; quoted in Osterhaven, *The Spirit of the Reformed Tradition,* p. 101.

3. This is found in the Presbyterian/Reformed *Hymnbook* (1955), the Christian Reformed *Psalter Hymnal* (1976), and the Orthodox Presbyterian *Trinity Hymnal* (1961); but it is missing in the more recent Presbyterian *Worshipbook* (1970). It is also in the new Reformed Church

(RCA) hymnal, *Rejoice in the Lord,* scheduled for publication by Eerdmans in 1984.

4. Roger R. Nicole, "In Better Words," *The Presbyterian Journal* (8 October 1975), p. 9.
   "There is a mighty effort in these Canons to safeguard the freedom and grace of God, and to distinguish the Christian religion from all self-help schemes," Plantinga, *A Place to Stand,* p. 136.

5. David H.C. Read, *Virginia Woolf Meets Charlie Brown* (Grand Rapids, Mich.: Eerdmans, 1968), p. 93.

6. Edward A. Dowey, Jr., *A Commentary on the Confession of 1967 and an Introduction to the Book of Confessions* (Philadelphia: Westminster Press, 1968), p. 269.

7. There are a few exceptions where scripture receives only passing attention, e.g., the *First Confession of Basel* (1534) and the *Scots Confession* of 1560.

8. Similar statements are found in the Gallican Confession, Article IV, and the *Second Helvetic Confession,* Chapter I. Later, Dutch Calvinists such as Herman Bavinck and Abraham Kuyper approved of this approach. See quotations in *Authority and Interpretation* by Rogers and McKim, pp. 389-90.

9. Harold Lindsell, *The Battle for the Bible* (Grand Rapids, Mich.: Zondervan, 1976). Cf. his sequel, *The Bible in the Balance,* which is largely a response to his critics (Grand Rapids, Mich.: Zondervan, 1979).

10. Lindsell, *Battle,* pp. 36-37.

11. Since Lindsell's attack centered on Fuller Theological Seminary, not surprisingly one of the first responses came from that source: *Biblical Authority,* ed. Jack Rogers, professor of philosophical theology at Fuller Seminary. Other contributors are well-known evangelicals such as Paul Rees, Clark Pinnock, Bernard Ramm, and David Hubbard (President of Fuller Seminary). The much larger, very scholarly sequel is *Authority and Interpretation,* Rogers and McKim.

12. Lester De Koster, Editorial, *The Banner* (November 19, 1976), p. 10.

13. The sixteenth-century Reformed confessions follow Calvin here, but the *Westminster Confession* introduces the notion of a covenant of works (VIII,2). Until fairly recently, this was accepted by conservative Reformed theologians (e.g., Louis Berkhof) but is now being repudiated by most Reformed theologians. See Murray, *Covenant of Grace.*

14. On the role of the covenant as an interpretive principle for the Westminster Divines, see Rogers and McKim, pp. 214-16.

15. Peter Meinhold, *Ökumenische Kirchenkunde* (Stuttgart: Kreuz-Verlag, 1962), p. 354.

16. His first and second attempts at drawing up a church constitution (variously called "Articles" and "Ordinances") can be found in *Calvin: Theological Treatises,* ed. J.K.S. Reid.

17. "Our [presbyterian] 400-year-old representative form of government,

combining the twin values of authority and freedom like cranapple juice—
so that authority doesn't become tyrannical, nor freedom fragmenting—is
high on the list of those characteristics that make us different from some
other members of the Christian family." James W. Angell, "A Special Way
of Believing," part of a special feature, "What Does It Mean to Be
Presbyterian?" in *United Presbyterian, A.D. 1981* 10 (June/July 1981),
p. 12.

18. Calvin had a fourth office, that of teacher, which today is rarely found in
Reformed Churches. The Reformed Church in America, however, still has
this fourth office, that of professor of theology. See Henderson, *The
Teaching Office.*

19. Osterhaven, *Spirit of the Reformed Tradition,* p. 65. Within the various
Reformed Churches, however, there is not always agreement as to the
nature of the office of elder. See Heideman, *Reformed Bishops and Catholic
Elders,* pp. 120ff.

20. Particularly in the Scottish Presbyterian Church, owing partially to the
peculiar political and economic situation there, the office of deacon
frequently was misunderstood or fell into disuse. In certain American
Presbyterian Churches the same is true. See Henderson, *Presbyterianism,*
pp. 81-88. "In the evolution of Presbyterian Church in the United States,
the deacons sometimes became more concerned with the business affairs of
the church than with the ministry of compassion" (Leith, *Introduction to
the Reformed Tradition,* p. 146.)

21. See Heideman, *Reformed Bishops and Catholic Elders,* ch. 7, "What Is a
Deacon?" Cf. *Service in Christ: Essays Presented to Karl Barth on His 80th
Birthday* (Grand Rapids, Mich.: Eerdmans, 1966), especially the opening
essay by T.F. Torrance, and those on Bucer by B. Hall, on Calvin by J.K.S.
Reid, and on *diakonia* in Reformed Churches today by J.L.M. Haire.

22. "The servant image is the most significant symbol in the Bible and in the
Christian religion" (John A. Mackay, "The Form of a Servant," in *The
Princeton Seminary Bulletin* 51 [June 1958], p. 30).
    The servant image was the theme of the World Alliance of Reformed
Churches international assembly in Brazil in 1959.

23. From "Presbyterianism" in *Encyclopedia Britannica,* fourteenth edition
(1967), 18:467; cited in Leith, *Introduction to the Reformed Tradition,*
p. 147.

24. Here, even the late John T. McNeill errs when he writes, "A third mark,
subordinate but important for Calvin, is discipline . . ." (*The History and
Character of Calvinism* [New York: Oxford University Press, 1954/1973],
p. 214). Jan Weerda suggests that discipline did not become a mark of the
church in the world for Calvin because he regarded it as enclosed in the
proclamation of the Word and the administration of the sacraments. "For
according to its proper meaning it is an application of the authority of the
Word of God which requires neither authority nor execution (*Handanle-*

gung)" ("Ordnung zur Lehre—zur Theologie der Kirchen-ordnung bei Calvin," in *Calvin Studien 1959*, ed. Jürgen Moltmann [Neukirchen: Neukirchen Kr. Moers, 1960], p. 168).

25. M.M. Knappen, in his monumental study *Tudor Puritanism*, cites the following Puritan claim: "We stand for the doctrine and discipline of the best Reformed churches." Knappen adds, "And the Anglican found it hard to refute this boast" (Chicago: The University of Chicago Press, 1939; Phoenix edition, 1966), p. 249.

26. See Eugene P. Heideman, "The Church and Christian Discipline," *Reformed Review* 16 (March 1963), pp. 32-33; R.N. Caswell, "Calvin and Church Discipline," in *John Calvin*, ed. G.E. Duffield (Grand Rapids, Mich.: Eerdmans, 1966), p. 211; and Osterhaven, pp. 54-55.

27. Karl Holl, *Gesammelte Aufsätze* 3 (Tübingen: J.C.B. Mohr, 1928/1964), p. 267.

28. See E. Harris Harbison, *Christianity and History* (Princeton, N.J.: Princeton University Press, 1964), ch. 11: "The Idea of Utility in the Thought of John Calvin."

29. Niesel, *The Gospel and the Churches*, p. 194.

30. Morton Enslin, "Religion without Theology," *Religion in Life* 45 (Spring 1976), p. 71.

31. Lutheran scholars are not agreed as to whether Luther taught a third use of the law, but it is taught in one of the Lutheran confessions, the *Formula of Concord* (1577), Article VI. See the balanced appraisal of Eugene F. Klug in *A Contemporary Look at the Formula of Concord*, ed. D. Preus and Wilbert H. Rosin (St. Louis: Concordia Publishing House, 1978), pp. 187ff.

32. See my discussion in *Guilt, Grace and Gratitude*, ed. Donald J. Bruggink, pp. 194ff.

33. It is extremely important to understand Calvin's doctrine of the *justification of works* in this connection. "We must remember that God 'accepts' believers by reason of works only because he is their source and graciously, by way of liberality, deigns also to show acceptance toward the good works he has himself bestowed" (III.17.5; cf. III.16.1 and III 17.3, 10).

34. Cf. the same phrase in ch. 13—"Of Sanctification"—in the *Westminster Confession*: By Christ's Word and Spirit dwelling in believers "the dominion of the whole body of sin is destroyed, and the several lusts thereof are *more and more* weakened and mortified, and they *more and more* quickened and strengthened, in all saving graces. . . ."

35. Note how Calvin relates election and holiness in III.22.1-3.

36. Cf. Bieler, *The Social Humanism of Calvin*, and Graham, *The Constructive Revolutionary*.

37. The first English translation of most of this classic appears in *Melanchthon and Bucer*, ed. Wilhelm Pauck (Philadelphia: Westminster Press, 1979). See Pauck's Introduction, pp. 155ff.

38. Pauck, *Melanchthon and Bucer*, p. 156.
39. See Perry Miller, *Errand into the Wilderness*, ch. 5, "The Puritan State and Puritan Society" (New York: Harper Torchbooks, 1964). Cf. Leith, *Introduction to the Reformed Tradition*, pp. 72-75.
40. Joseph Haroutunian, *Piety Versus Moralism: The Passing of New England Theology* (New York: Harper Torchbook, 1970; first edition 1932), p. 88.
41. Kuyper, *Lectures on Calvinism*.
42. Ibid., p. 49.
43. See also Gordon Spykman, "Sphere-Sovereignty."
44. English translation published by New Brunswick Theological Seminary, New Jersey, in 1955.
45. Published in *Theology Today* 11 (October 1954), p. 374. The Genevan Calvin scholar and pastor, Andre Bieler, concludes his fine little book *The Social Humanism of Calvin* (Richmond, Va.: John Knox Press, 1964), p. 71, on a similar, salutary note:

> Of all the Christian confessions, Calvinism is the most ecumenical because of this fundamental reason: Calvinism has never been enclosed in a rigid, absolute, and final definition of its tenets. Calvinism has always proclaimed that the only authority of the church is the Bible which witnesses to Christ who himself is the Word of God and the sovereign authority—the living authority to which the church is submitted. The church therefore never possesses a truth of her own. All the church can do is to let herself be led ever anew and be re-formed by this only truth which is the living Christ—the eternal Christ who by his Holy Spirit is active in human history.

Index

Ahlstrom, Sydney, 33
Alexander, Archibald, 127
Ames, William, 136
Amyraut, Moise, 34
Anabaptism, 7, 80, 102
Anglican Communion, 8, 22, 83
Apostles' Creed, 12
Architecture, church, 139
Aristotle, 33
Arminianism:
  in church music, 27, 29
  orthodox Calvinism opposed
    to, 60n, 94
  theology of, 27n, 95
Art, 68-70, 110
Augsburg Confession, 11, 97
Augustine of Hippo, St., 33
  on free will, 46, 94n
  influence on Calvinism, 45, 95
  on predestination, 39, 42

Baptism, 76, 95
Baptists:
  connections with the
    Reformed tradition, 8, 124
  and confessions, 9, 14
  and the Holy Spirit, 73, 74, 84
  and liturgy, 22
  and schism, 86
Barmen Confession, 12
Barth, Karl, 1, 2, 11, 28, 33
Basel, 5
Battles, Ford Lewis, 8
Bavinck, Herman, 37, 38, 60, 110
Beethoven, Ludwig van, 48
Belgic Confession, 9, 13, 100
  on the church, 18, 92

on scripture, 10, 97, 98, 99, 101
  on the Holy Spirit, 99, 101
Benoit, Jean-Daniel, 36
Berkhof, Hendrikus, 37
  on the Holy Spirit, 76, 78, 80
Berkhof, Louis, 8, 33
Berkouwer, G.C., 37, 38, 41, 80
Bern, 5
Beza, Theodore, 19n, 27, 32, 94
Bible Presbyterian Church, 85
Blake, Eugene Carson, 87
Bloesch, Donald, 35
Bonhoeffer, Dietrich, 52
The Book of Concord, 11
Book of Confessions (Southern
  Presbyterian Church), 13
Book of Confessions (United
  Presbyterian Church), 11
Bourgeois, Louis, 27
Brueggeman, Walter, 62
Bruggink, Donald J., 139
Brunner, Emil, 33
Bucer, Martin, 6
  on the church, 18, 89, 105
  influence on Calvin, 18, 94,
    106, 109
Bullinger, Heinrich:
  and church unity, 90, 91
  and Reformed tradition, 40,
    90, 94
  theology of, 57

Calvin, John, 1, 6, 93
  church order of, 17-18, 103,
    104-5
  and church unity, 17-18, 86,
    88-91

on civil government, 68, 109
and covenant, 57, 102
and depravity, 46, 47-48, 50
on grace, 96
on the Holy Spirit, 74-77, 78,
   100-101
on law, 51-56
and music, 26, 27, 29
on preaching, 25-26
on predestination, 39-42, 43
role in the Reformation, 5,
   90-91, 98, 103
role in the Reformed tradition,
   1, 3, 57, 98
on sacraments, 22-24
on scholastic theology, 32, 33,
   34, 37, 38, 106
on scripture, 97, 98, 99,
   100-101, 102
on worship, 21, 27, 37
works:
   Genevan Catechism, 40
   Genevan Psalter, 26, 27-28
   *Institutes of the Christian
      Religion,* 26, 36-37, 68,
      75
   The Instruction in Faith,
      40
Canons of Dort, 9, 13
on covenant, 60
and depravity, 46, 49
TULIP in, 93. *See also* Synod
   of Dort TULIP
Carnell, Edward John, 34
Carter, Jimmy, 65
Charismatic gifts, 78-84
Charismatic renewal, 78
Christian Reformed Church:
   Dutch heritage of, 5, 8
   government of, 17
   hymnals in, 27, 28
   liturgy in, 29

and schism, 85
schools in, 58-59
Church reunions, in the
   Reformed tradition, 86
Church of Scotland:
   legalism in, 52
   origins of, 6, 7, 19
   schism in, 85
   and *Westminster Confession,* 10
   worship in, 21, 27
Cicero, Marcus Tullius, 48
Clark, Gordon, 34, 35
Coccejus, Johannes, 57
Cochrane, Arthur, 11, 62
Come, Arnold, 78
Confession of 1967 (United
   Presbyterian Church), 12, 13
Confessions, Reformed, 3, 9-15
Congregational Christian
   Church, 86
   and Reformed tradition, 8, 9,
      124
Consensus Tigurinus, 90
Council of Trent, 90
Covenant theology, 57-62, 102
Covenanters, 27, 85
Cranmer, Thomas, Archbishop,
   19, 91
Cumberland Presbyterian
   Church, 85
Cyprian of Carthage, St., 76

Daane, James, 131
De Koster, Lester, 100
A Declaration of Faith (Southern
   Presbyterian Church), 13
Depravity. *See* Total depravity
Dickinson, Helen, 29
*The Doctrine Concerning Holy
   Scriptures* (Netherlands
   Reformed Church), 13
Dodd, C.H., 41

Dooyeweerd, H., 110
Doumergue, Emile, 18, 97
Dowey, E.A., 97
Duff, Alexander, 87
Durant, Will, 48
Dutch Reformed Churches. *See* Christian Reformed Church; Netherlands Reformed Church; Reformed Church in America

Ecclesiology, 17-20, 76, 103-5
Ecumenism, 85-92
Edward VI (king of England), 91, 109
Edwards, Jonathan, 42, 77
Eichrodt, Walther, 57
Einstein, Albert, 48
England, Reformed tradition in, 7, 19, 27
Enslin, Morton, 107
Episcopal Church. *See* Anglican Communion
Evangelical and Reformed Church, 86
Evangelical Synod of North America, 86

Falwell, Jerry, 65
Farel, Guillaume, 5, 94
Federal theology, 59-60
Five points of Calvinism. *See* TULIP
Formula of Concord, 39, 53n
Foundations and Perspectives of Confession (Netherlands Reformed Church), 13, 111
France, Reformed Church in, 5, 7, 27
Freedom, Christian, 55-56
Frelinghuysen, Theodorus Jacobus, 77

Fundamentalism, 14, 65

Gaffin, Richard, Jr., 79
Gallican Confession, 97, 98
Geisler, Norman, 35
Geneva, 5
    Calvin's role in, 68, 109
    church order in, 17-18, 103
    liturgy in, 21
    public discipline in, 51
Genevan Catechism, 40
Genevan Confession, 9, 97
Genevan Psalter, 26, 28
Gerhard, Johann, 32
Germany, Reformed churches in, 5, 7, 52
Gerstner, John, 34
Gogh, Vincent van, 48
Gomarus (Francis Gomar), 60
Grace, Reformed theology of, 94-97
Groen, George, 58

Hageman, Howard, 22
Haller, Berthold, 5
Harmelink, Herman, III, 87
Hegel, G.W.F., 33
Heidelberg Catechism, 7, 9, 12, 21
    and covenant, 57
    on faith, 96, 106
    on human depravity, 47
    on law, 55, 107-8
    on predestination, 40
    on reason, 37
    on word and Spirit, 101
Heideman, Eugene, 14, 131
Henderson, G.D., 19
Hendry, George S., 78
Henry, Carl F.H., 34-35
Heppe, H.L., 97
Heuvel, Albert van den, 87
Heyer, George S., 69

Hodge, A.A., 60
Hodge, Charles, 8, 12, 33-34
    on covenant, 60
    on scripture, 97
Hoekema, Anthony, 79
Holiness Churches, 9, 22, 83
Holl, Karl, 106
Holy Spirit:
    and reason, 35
    Reformed theology of, 73-84,
        100-101
    and scripture, 99, 101
Huddleston, Trevor, 59
Hughes, Philip, 8
Hungary, Reformed churches in,
    7, 19
Hunter, A.M., 41, 97

Institutes of the Christian Religion.
    See Calvin, John
The Instruction in Faith. See
    Calvin, John
International Council of
    Christian Churches, 1, 86
Ireland, Reformed tradition in, 7
Italy, Reformed churches in, 7

Jacobs, Paul, 39
Jansenism, 45
Jewett, Paul K., 54

Kant, Immanuel, 33
Kierkegaard, Soren, 33
Klooster, Fred, 131
Knox, John, 6, 19, 94
    on the church, 105
    on gifts of the Holy Spirit, 78
    on sacraments, 22, 23
Kraemer, Hendrik, 87
Kuyper, Abraham, 71
    on Christianity and society, 58,
        64n, 70, 110

    on covenant, 58, 60
    on the Holy Spirit, 77

Lara-Braud, Jorge, 62
Lasco, Johannes à, 7
Lausanne, 5
Leeuw, Gerardus van der, 29, 68
Legalism, in the Reformed
    tradition, 51-56, 107
Leith, John, 17, 19
Lindsell, Harold, 34, 35, 99
Liturgy, in the Reformed
    Church, 21-30
    theology and, 29-30
Liturgy of the Reformed Church in
    the Palatinate, 21
Lombard, Peter, 32
Lord's Supper, Reformed
    theology of, 23-24, 76
Luther, Martin, 5, 29, 46, 74, 76
    on predestination, 39
    and scholastic theology, 32, 33
    and secular society, 48, 109
    theology of, 46, 53n, 56, 76,
        102
Lutheran Church-Missouri
    Synod, 11
Lutherans:
    in the charismatic renewal, 83
    ecclesiology of, 103, 105
    emphasis on justification, 97,
        107-8
    and liturgy, 22
    in the Reformation, 5, 7, 89-90
    and scholasticism, 32
    and schism, 86

Mackay, John, 87
    on Calvin's piety, 38
    on church unity, 87, 92, 112
Marcion, 102
Marot, Clement, 27

McCord, James I., 2, 30
McIntyre, Carl, 1, 2, 86
McKim, Donald, 34
McNeill, John T., 19, 36
Meinhold, Peter, 103, 105
Melanchthon, Philip, 90, 91
Melville, Andrew, 19
Menninger, Karl, 45
Mennonites, 7
Methodism, 9, 74
    Arminianism and, 27
    and the work of the Holy
        Spirit, 73, 74, 83, 84
Moltmann, Jürgen, 62
Montanism, 80
Montgomery, John Warwick, 34,
    35
Moral Majority, 65-66
Mudge, Lewis, 74
Murray, John, 60
Music, in the Reformed Church,
    25, 26-30

National Council of Churches,
    65
Netherlands Reformed Church,
    6, 7
    confessions in, 12, 13
    legalism in, 52
    renewal in, 77
    schism in, 85
    worship in, 27
Newbigin, Lesslie, 80, 87
Niebuhr, H. Richard, 46, 48
Niesel, Wilhelm, 1, 2, 19
Noordmans, O., 78

O'Connor, Edward, 82
Ockham, John of, 33
Oecolampadius, Johannes, 5, 94
Orthodox Presbyterian Church,
    27, 28, 85

Osterhaven, M.E., 14, 104
Our Song of Hope (Reformed
    Church in America), 13-14,
    70, 111

Packer, James I., 8, 43
Parker, T.H.L., 8
Pascal, Blaise, 45
Pelagianism, 94
Pentecostalism, 74, 80-81
    on confessions, 14
    on the Holy Spirit, 73, 82,
        83-84
    on sanctification, 76
Pieters, Albertus, 60, 97
Pietism, 52, 77
    on the Holy Spirit, 78
    on secular affairs, 48, 65
Pinnock, Clark, 34
Plantinga, Cornelius, 49
Plato, 33, 48
Poissy, Colloquy of, 91
Poland, Reformed churches in, 7,
    19
Politics, Reformed tradition and,
    65-68, 109-10
Polman, A.D.R., 131
Preaching, in the Reformed
    Church, 25-26
Predestination, doctrine of,
    39-44, 51
Presbyterian Church in America,
    86
Presbyterian Church in U.S.
    (Southern), 13, 85
Presbyterian Church of North
    America, 86
Presbyterian Church U.S., 86
Presbyterian Church, Scottish.
    See Church of Scotland
Presbyterians, 7, 19, 83, 124. *See
    also names of specific churches*

Princeton school theology, 35
Princeton Theological Seminary, 2, 30, 87, 112, 127
Protestant Reformed Church, 85
Protestant Orthodoxy, 33, 77
Puritanism, 52, 124
　on the Holy Spirit, 78
　theology of, 42, 48, 109

Quakerism, 80
Quenstedt, J.A., 32

Rationalism, and Reformed theology, 31-38
Reformed Church in America, 2, 87, 111
　confessions in, 13-14, 111
　Dutch heritage of, 5, 8
　government of, 17
　hymnals in, 27, 28
　liturgy in, 22, 29
　schism in, 85
Reformed Church in the United States (German), 86
Reformed Presbyterian Church, Evangelical Synod, 86
Reformed Presbyterian Church (Covenanters), 27, 85
Reid, J.K.S., 97
Richardson, Herbert, 70
Ridderbos, Herman, 131
Rogers, Jack B., 34
Roman Catholic Church, 30, 83, 90, 91
Rottenberg, Isaac, 67
Ruler, A.A. van, 14, 71, 78
　on Christianity and secular activities, 67, 70, 110
Runner, H. Evan, 33

Sabbatarianism, 52, 54-55
Sacraments, 76, 105

Sanctification, 76, 106-8
Schaeffer, Francis, 34, 35
Schaff, Philip, 31
Schelling, F.W.J. von, 33
Schism, in Reformed tradition, 85-86, 87
Schleiermacher, Friedrich, 1
Scholasticism, medieval, 31-32
Scholasticism, Protestant, 32, 33, 35, 38, 98
Science, Reformed Christians and, 70, 110
Scofield Reference Bible, 60
Scotland, Reformed tradition in. *See* Church of Scotland
Scottish Realism, 33-34, 38
Scotus, John Duns, 33
Scripture, authority of, 9-10, 97-102
Second Helvetic Confession, 12, 23, 26, 40, 97
Secular affairs, Reformed tradition and, 63-71
Seeberg, R., 97
Seerveld, Calvin, 69
Servetus, Michael, 51
South Africa, Reformed Church in, 59
Sproul, R.C., 34
Stewart, John W., 34
Strasbourg, 6, 21
Strong, Augustus Hopkins, 8
Swiss Reformed Church, 5, 7, 11
　worship in, 22, 27
Synod of Dort, 27n, 45n, 60n. *See also* Canons of Dort TULIP

Tennent, Gilbert, 77
Thomas Aquinas, St., 32, 33
Tillich, Paul, 33
Torrance, Thomas F., 37, 70, 126

Total depravity, doctrine of, 45-50
Trinterud, L.J., 104
TULIP (five points of Calvinism), 27n, 45n, 93, 95
Turretin, Francis, 32, 33, 34

United Church of Christ, 86
United Presbyterian Church, 86
United Presbyterian Church, U.S.A.:
  and church reunion, 86
  confessions in, 11, 13
  theology in, 2
United States, Reformed tradition in, 7, 27, 52. *See also names of specific churches*
Ursinus, Zacharius, 57

Van Dusen, Henry, 80
Van Til, Cornelius, 1, 34
Viret, Pierre, 5
Visser 't Hooft, W.A., 1, 2, 87
Voetius, Gisbert, 32
Vollenhoven, D., 110

Waldensians, 7
Warfield, B.B., 34, 78, 97
Watts, Isaac, 29
Wernle, Paul, 56
Wesley, John, 76

Wesleyanism. *See* Methodism
Western Seminary, 8
Westminster Catechisms, 12, 37, 57, 58
Westminster Confession, 9, 12
  on the church, 92
  covenant theology in, 58, 60
  on depravity, 46
  on scripture, 97, 98, 99
Westminster Directory, 21
Westminster Seminary, 1
Whitefield, George, 77
Williams, Charles, 42
Wollebius, Johannes, 32
Wolterstorff, Nicholas, 69
Woolley, Paul, 15
World Alliance of Presbyterian and Reformed Churches, 1, 61, 112
World Council of Churches, 1, 87

Zurich, 5n, 6, 25, 40
Zwingli, Ulrich:
  on charismatic gifts, 78
  on covenant, 57, 102
  followers of, 89, 90
  and preaching, 25
  and Reformed tradition, 5, 6, 94
  on sacraments, 22